WORKBOOK
Teacher's Edition

Time to Wonder

Level 13

Bernard J. Weiss
Loreli Olson Steuer

Holt
Basic
Reading

HOLT, RINEHART AND WINSTON, PUBLISHERS
New York • Toronto • London • Sydney

Copyright © 1980, 1977, 1973 by Holt, Rinehart and Winston, Publishers
All Rights Reserved
Printed in the United States of America

ISBN 0-03-048021-3
0123   111   98765432

Photo Credits:

page 46   American Foundation for the Blind;
page 66   Johnson Publishers;
page 109   New York Public Library.

Cover illustration by Gil Cohen.

Table of Contents

This Workbook can be used with the 1977 Pupil's Edition as well as the 1980 Pupil's Edition.
When the stories in these two editions differ, both the 1977 title and the 1980 title are listed.
Simply refer to the story title that applies to the Pupil's Edition your class is using, and assign the
corresponding Workbook pages.

Recipes for Laughter

Underline the phrase that best completes each of the sentences.

1. The humorous events in the story come about partly because the weather is
  a. hot and muggy.
  b. cold and snowy.
  c. <u>rainy and windy.</u>

2. We laugh at the children's method of cooking because they
  a. behave just like expert cooks.
  b. <u>pay no attention to the amounts they use.</u>
  c. move around so slowly.

3. Two of the surprising and funny ingredients the children use are
  a. marshmallows and cinnamon.
  b. corn syrup and chocolate squares.
  c. <u>lemonade and hot sauce.</u>

4. We laugh again when the children first taste the candy because they
  a. <u>gasp, choke, and snort.</u>
  b. can't stop eating it.
  c. give it all away to the neighbors.

5. At the end of the story we are both surprised and amused when Alvin
  a. gives up cooking for good.
  b. <u>wins a prize for his candy.</u>
  c. begins concocting a new recipe.

Reread pages 26-28. Then, decide which of the words on the right best describe Alvin as he writes his recipe. Write the letter of the words in the sentence blank.

1. Alvin is like ____c____ when he tries to remember exactly how the candy was made.

a. an expert cook

2. Alvin is like ____b____ when he makes up the ingredients and amounts he can't remember.

b. an inventor

3. Alvin is like ____a____ when he uses terms like "two pinches to taste" in his instructions.

c. a newspaper reporter

Which of the words above best describe how Alvin wrote his recipe? __an inventor__

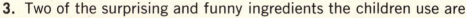

Why? __Alvin made up more than he remembered; the cooking terms were "picked__

__up" from his mother's cookbooks.__

Level 13: "The Magnificent Brain Concocts a Recipe" pp. 16-29.
Objectives: To identify humorous elements in metaphors and similes. (Comprehension)

1

Sounds and Letters: There's More Than Meets the Eye

Turn to the Full Pronunciation Key on page 490 of your textbook. Then complete the following paragraph with the words below.

sound	spelling	words	box
twice	41	26	parentheses

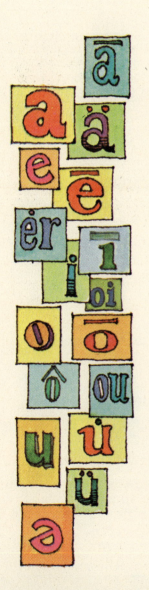

Can you explain why most dictionaries and glossaries have a Pronunciation Key? Let's see if you can figure it out. How many letters are in our alphabet? __26__. How many separate sounds are represented by the Pronunciation Key? __41__. As you can see there are nearly __twice__ as many English speech sounds as there are letters in the alphabet. The Pronunciation Key, on the other hand, is designed to have one separate symbol for each English __sound__. Because many of these symbols resemble alphabet letters, we will place them in a __box__ so they will be easy to recognize. In a glossary or dictionary the symbols are often written between __parentheses__ when they follow an entry word. Pronunciation Key symbols help us pronounce unfamiliar __words__, and they also help us when we are studying the various __spelling__ patterns for each English speech sound.

Level 13: "The Magnificent Brain Concocts a Recipe" pp. 16-29.

Objectives: To recognize that there are more vowel sounds than vowel letters in English. (Decoding/Encoding Skills) To describe the purpose and uses of the Pronunciation Key. (Study Skills)

One Letter May Stand for More Than One Speech Sound.

Using the Pronunciation Key on page 490 of your text, put a check after each pronunciation symbol that represents the sound of the underlined letter. The first example is done for you.

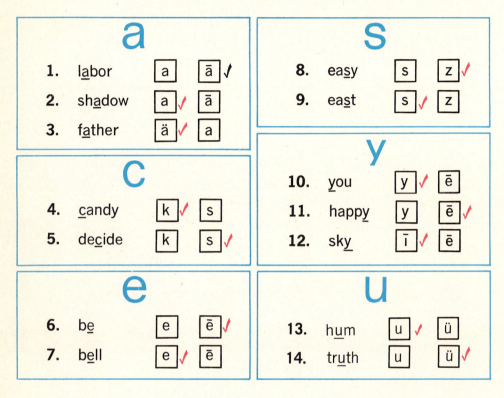

a

1. labor   a   ā ✓
2. shadow   a ✓   ā
3. father   ä ✓   a

c

4. candy   k ✓   s
5. decide   k   s ✓

e

6. be   e   ē ✓
7. bell   e ✓   ē

s

8. easy   s   z ✓
9. east   s ✓   z

y

10. you   y ✓   ē
11. happy   y   ē ✓
12. sky   ī ✓   ē

u

13. hum   u ✓   ü
14. truth   u   ü ✓

And One Speech Sound May Be Spelled by Two or More Letters.

As you can see from the first example below, one or more letters can stand for a single sound. Underline the letters in each word that represent the sound of the Pronunciation Key symbol in the box.

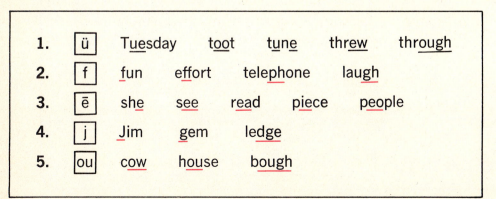

1. ü   Tuesday   toot   tune   threw   through
2. f   fun   effort   telephone   laugh
3. ē   she   see   read   piece   people
4. j   Jim   gem   ledge
5. ou   cow   house   bough

3

Find pages 8-13 in your textbook. Then complete the following sentences by underlining the correct answer. The first one is done for you.

Time to Wonder

1. These six pages are called the Index—the Table of Contents—the Glossary

2. The purpose of this section is to list the parts of the book in alphabetical order — by page number — in order of importance

3. Our book is divided into 5—6—7 units.

4. The title of each unit is printed before—after—alongside of the story titles.

5. The title of each selection is immediately followed by the page number—the kind of selection and the author—unit number

6. The name of the author is followed by the page number—the main character—the kind of selection

Each unit of our book contains selections that relate to specific subject areas. Skim through the story titles and illustrations in each unit and see if you can write the correct **unit number** and **title** by each of the descriptions below.

SUBJECT	UNIT	TITLE
SOCIAL STUDIES: **TRAVEL BY LAND, SEA, AND AIR**	6	TO CATCH THE HIGH WINDS
SCIENCE: **THE ANIMAL KINGDOM**	3	THE WONDER OF LIFE
FINE ARTS: **MUSIC, PAINTING, DRAMA**	4	A DIFFERENT DRUMMER
COMMUNICATION: **OUR GREATEST INVENTION**	2	THE GIFT OF LANGUAGE
CLASSICAL LITERATURE: **FOLKTALES AND FAIRY TALES**	5	A WORLD OF WONDERS
MODERN LITERATURE: **STORIES ABOUT YOU AND ME**	1	BOOKS WILL VENTURE

Level 13: "The Magnificent Brain Concocts a Recipe" pp. 16-29.

Objective: To describe the form and function of the Table of Contents. (Study Skills)

Truth and Truth Stretching

Underline the phrase below that best describes how Periwinkle Jones talked about the things that happened to her.

a. told only facts   **b.** exaggerated facts   **c.** mixed up facts

Read the following sentences. Then write how Periwinkle Jones might describe these same events.

1. The honeysuckle grew six feet tall. It spread itself almost thickly enough to hide under.

   Answers will vary.

   _____

2. The old-time cars would heat up so much that the drivers would have to pull over to the side of the road and ask for water.

   _____

   _____

   _____

3. You will find a treasure in those fields if you work hard, and the treasure will be good crops.

   _____

   _____

   _____

4. There was only a hole that was not very deep where the men had been digging. _____

   _____

   _____

5. The men had been digging for worms to go fishing in the early morning. _____

   _____

   _____

Choose one of the titles below. On a separate sheet of paper write two paragraphs. In the first, use factual details of what might really happen. In the second, use exaggerated details of what would probably never happen. Answers will vary.

A Walk in a Rainstorm   **A Noise in the Attic**   **A Mouse in the Classroom**

Level 13: "Periwinkle Jones" pp. 32-42.

Objective: To supply examples of exaggeration. (Comprehension)

SENTENCE WORD ORDER

Look at the groups of words below. Some are sentences, and some are not because the words are not in the right order. Put an **S** on the line before a sentence. Put an **N** before any group of words that is not a sentence.

N	**1.** in lived Periwinkle California	S	**6.** there was a tapping sound
S	**2.** the two boys rocked lazily	N	**7.** two digging men were
N	**3.** arrived Periwinkle night last	N	**8.** going fishing men the two were
S	**4.** one boy kicked the floor	N	**9.** all around history was them
N	**5.** Oscar well about talked the	S	**10.** the men heard a noise

Rewrite the groups of words that are sentences using the correct capitalization and punctuation. Reorder the other groups of words to make sentences. Write them correctly.

1. Periwinkle lived in California.

2. The two boys rocked lazily.

3. Periwinkle arrived last night.

4. One boy kicked the floor.

5. Oscar talked about the well.

6. There was a tapping sound.

7. Two men were digging.

8. The two men were going fishing.

9. History was all around them.

10. The men heard a noise.

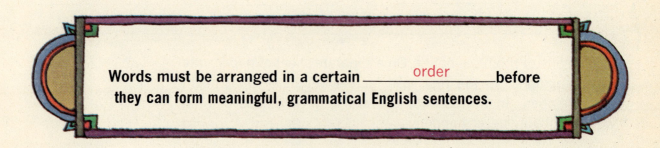

Words must be arranged in a certain ___order___ before they can form meaningful, grammatical English sentences.

Level 13: "Periwinkle Jones" pp. 32-42.

Objectives: To distinguish between sentences and groups of words in random order. To reorder groups of words into sentences. (Language) To use capital letters and periods in statements. (Language)

GLOSSARY (glos′ə rē) a list of special words...

Find the Glossary in your book. Then write in the correct answers or underline the blue words or phrases that are the correct answers.

1. The guide words on page 491 are ___abacus___ and ___apartment (antibiotic)___.

   They help you locate other words on the page because <u>they are the first and last words on each page</u>—they relate to the meaning of the other words on the page.

2. If the guide words on a Glossary page were *fire* and *fox*, which of the words below would be found on the same page?

   <u>fountain</u>   festival   fair   final   <u>fool</u>   <u>first</u>

3. Find Latin in the Glossary. What are the guide words on that page? ___
   ___incubator-magnify (jungle-midge)___

   Find trough. What are the guide words on that page? ___
   ___till-yucca (theory-zucchini)___

4. Several kinds of information are given for each word in the Glossary. The first information is its correct spelling. The second is its <u>pronunciation</u>—definition

5. The Full Pronunciation Key is found on page 490, but a Short Pronunciation Key is also found at the top—<u>bottom</u> of each <u>left-hand</u>—right-hand page.

6. Use the guide words to find: *citizen, census, composer*.

   a. What page are these words on? ___494___

   b. What are the guide words for that page? ___
   ___cancellation mark-Congress (cablegram-composer)___

   c. Write the three words in alphabetical order. After each word, write its correct number of syllables.
   ___census (2); citizen (3); composer (3).___

   d. Which syllable is stressed first in citizen? ___first___

   e. Is the first e in <u>petrified</u> pronounced the same as the <u>e</u> in <u>me</u> or <u>men</u>?
   ___men___

Level 13: "Periwinkle Jones" pp. 32-42.

Objectives: To identify guide words in the Glossary. To use the Glossary to determine the pronunciation of words. To describe and use common features of the Glossary. (Study Skills)

Finding Clues to Word Meaning

Read the sentences below and answer the questions that follow.

> In one of them was a nestful of blue jay **fledglings.**

1. Find this sentence in the story and read the complete paragraph. Then tell which of the following words gives the closest meaning to **fledgling.** ___c___

a. eggs **b.** feathers **c.** baby birds

2. One of the clues in the paragraph that helps us guess the meaning of **fledgling** is "still-weak claws." What are some others? "half-grown wings," "teetered and clutched the rim," etc.

> "And I've got the best aim in the whole school, too," he **boasted.**

3. Find and read this sentence in its complete paragraph context in the story. Then tell which of the following words seems to give the closest meaning to **boasted?** ___a___

a. bragged **b.** argued **c** complained

4. What are some of the things Reggie is doing in this paragraph that help us discover the word's meaning? Prancing, grinning proudly, saying, "I've got the best aim."

> Reggie bent down and **gingerly** scooped up the bird in his hands.

5. Find and read this sentence and its complete paragraph in the story. Which of the following words gives the closest meaning of **gingerly** in this sentence? ___b___

a. quickly **b.** carefully **c.** roughly

6. Write the sentence that tells why Reggie had to handle the bird a certain way. "Its head wobbled loosely."

> "No, you great big **spoiled** baby!" said Reggie.

7. Read this sentence and its complete paragraph in the story. Which of the following words gives the closest meaning to **spoiled** in this sentence? ___a___

a. pampered **b.** cute **c.** weak

8. From the rest of the paragraph how would you describe what a person does who is not spoiled? Gets things for himself, acts grown-up, etc.

9. Write the dictionary definition of **spoiled** that best describes its meaning in this sentence. Answers will vary depending on dictionary used.

8

Level 13: "The Boy Who Changed His Mind" pp. 44-55.

Objective: To use context clues to develop the meanings of words in a selection. (Comprehension)

Who's Who?

MAJOR CHARACTERS

The action in a fictional story centers on the **major,** or main, characters. These characters are described in more detail than any other characters in the story. As a story develops, the reader learns a lot about how these characters think, feel, and act in different situations.

Below are descriptions of the two major characters from Nellie Burchardt's "The Boy Who Changed His Mind." Write the name of the character described in each statement. Then decide whether the statement tells about the character's thoughts, feelings or actions. Put a **T** before each statement that tells a thought, an **F** before each that tells a feeling and an **A** before each statement that describes an action. Some statements may need more than one letter.

_____A_____ 1. He picked up a crushed tin can lying beside a waste basket and threw it at the birds. _____Reggie_____

_____A_____ 2. He did a dance around the tree. _____Reggie_____

_____A_____ 3. It lifted its head weakly. Its eyes stayed closed. _____Charley_____

_____T_____ 4. Suddenly he wished he had never heard of tin cans or blue jays. ___Reggie___

_____T_____ 5. Now why on earth had he taken the bird and what was he going to do with it? He really didn't know. _____Reggie_____

_____A,F___ 6. He went wild. Angrily he struck out at the hands that held him. ___Charley___

_____A_____ 7. He opened his beak wide and gave his baby cry for food. ____Charley_____

_____F_____ 8. His heart sank. _____Reggie_____

MINOR CHARACTERS

In the space below, list the names of all the other characters who are mentioned in the story. These are the **minor** characters. If you need to skim through the story to find their names, do so.

Joey, Diane, Mrs. Sullivan, Mr. Santino

What minor role does each character play in the story?

Joey—Reggie's friend, Diane—one of the girls, Mrs. Sullivan—

Reggie's teacher, and Mr. Santino—Reggie's neighbor who helps him

build a house for Charley.

Level 13: "The Boy Who Changed His Mind" pp. 44-45.

Objectives: To distinguish between major and minor characters and identify their roles in the story. (Comprehension)

9

WHICH SCHOOL?

Read each phrase in the box below. Then decide if it describes a school of the future or a school of today. Write the words under the proper headings. Some words belong in both columns.

1. one teacher, one pupil
2. one teacher, many pupils
3. write answers on paper
4. a punch code for answers
5. a human teacher
6. a mechanical teacher
7. children read
8. geography and history
9. homework and test papers
10. school in a special building
11. school in a pupil's home
12. put homework in a slot
13. give homework to human teacher
14. learn about fractions

Margie's and Tommy's Schools	**Our Schools**
one teacher, one pupil	one teacher, many pupils
a punch code for answers	write answers on paper
children read	a human teacher
a mechanical teacher	children read
geography and history	geography and history
school in a pupil's home	school in a special building
homework and test papers	homework and test papers
put homework in a slot	give homework to human teacher
learn about fractions	learn about fractions

1. What things would you like about Margie's and Tommy's schools? Answers will vary.

2. What things wouldn't you like? _____

3. Why did Margie think that the "old schools" were more fun? The children learned together. They could help one another and talk about it, etc.

4. Why do you agree or disagree? _____

Level 13: "The Fun They Had" pp. 58-63.
Objective: To identify and compare settings. (Comprehension)

Contrasting Characters

Sometimes an author will create two very different characters and weave their lives together in a story. This is the author's way of using contrast. The result is usually a story that is more interesting, exciting, and surprising for the reader. For example, in "The Fun They Had," contrast was used in the characters of Margie and Tommy. They were close friends, yet they were very different kinds of people.

Pictured below are these and other characters from stories you have read. Read the description given for each of the characters pictured in the left-hand column. List contrasting words which could be used to describe each of the characters in the right-hand column.

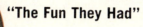

"The Fun They Had"

Tommy

1. A thirteen-year-old

2. A boy

3. Acts like a know-it-all

Margie

1. An eleven-year-old

2. A girl

3. Asks a lot of questions

"The Magnificent Brain Concocts a Recipe"

Alvin

1. Called "The Magnificent Brain"

2. Has a quick, active mind

Shoie

1. Called "The Great Athlete"

2. Has an active body

"Periwinkle Jones"

Periwinkle

1. A California girl

2. Talks quickly

3. Finds life exciting

Oscar

1. An Oklahoma boy

2. Speaks with a drawl

3. Finds life dull

Level 13: "The Fun They Had" pp. 58-63.

Objective: To identify contrast as one form of literary device. (Comprehension)

Word Arithmetic

Write in the missing words.

work + book = <u>   workbook   </u>   play + ground = <u>   playground   </u>

A word that is made by adding two words together is called a <u> compound </u> **word.**

Make eight common English compound words by adding **A** words to **B** words.

A.
up	book	spoon	nick	father	room	mate	some	string

B.

1. <u>   </u>something   4. cook<u>book</u>   7. tea<u>spoon</u>

2. school<u>room (-mate)</u>   5. play<u>mate (-room)</u>   8. <u>up</u>stairs

3. <u>nick</u>name   6. shoe<u>string</u>   9. grand<u>father</u>

Choose five of these compound words and use them in original sentences.

1. _____

2. _____

3. _____

4. _____

5. _____

Level 13: "The Fun They Had" pp. 58-63.

Objectives: To identify compound words. To construct and use compound words. (Language Skills)

"The Fun They Had":
Ideas and Action

A. Answer the questions below by putting a check in front of the correct answer.

1. Read page 58 of "The Fun They Had." Then decide which of the following sentences best sums up the **main idea** of the page.

_____**a.** The date is "May 17, 2157."

✔_____**b.** Tommy has found "a real book."

_____**c.** The book Tommy finds has "yellow and crinkly pages."

2. Read the paragraph on page 60 beginning with "The Inspector had smiled . . ." Which sentence below best states the main idea of the paragraph?

_____**a.** The Inspector smiled and patted Margie's head twice.

_____**b.** The Inspector slowed the geography sector of the mechanical teacher.

✔_____**c.** The Inspector explained it was the machine—and not Margie—that was at fault.

3. Read all of page 63. Which of these sentences best summarizes the main idea of the page?

✔_____**a.** Margie thought about the fun the kids must have had in the old schools.

_____**b.** The old schools had people for teachers.

_____**c.** Margie should have been learning her fractions.

B. Read the sentence below and each of the words following. Then underline all the words that would give the sentence meaning.

In Margie's dream, she _____ the mechanical teacher out the window.

<u>threw</u>   quickly   over   <u>booted</u>   <u>pushed</u>   book

The words you underlined should all be *verbs*. Do verbs usually *name, describe,* or *show*

action in the sentence? _____

What other verbs could be used in this sentence? _____

kicked, tossed, hurled, shoved, dropped

_____

Level 13: "The Fun They Had" pp. 58-63.

Objectives: To identify main ideas in a selection. (Comprehension) To identify verbs as words that show action. (Language Skills)

Words and Meaning in Miss Kirby's Room

Underline the word (or words) following the sentences below that come closest in meaning to the underlined word in the sentence as it is used in the story.

1. "Hank Yurchenko, the <u>hardest</u> hitter in Mrs. Otto's room, came up to the plate."

   <u>most powerful</u>   most difficult   most like iron

2. "Caught on the left <u>handlebar</u> by a little key chain was a white rabbit's foot."

   part of a bicycle   part of an animal trap   <u>pony tail</u>

3. "Feet <u>shuffled</u>, throats were cleared, and a pencil or two dropped. Several sneezes were heard."

   <u>moved nervously</u>   stamped loudly   danced in slow rhythm

4. "Susan felt a nasty little stab of <u>jealousy</u>."

   anger   <u>envy</u>   pain

5. "Susan realized that quite a few of the boys and girls had made it <u>plain</u> to Jamie that day that they didn't want her around."

   boring   painful   <u>clear</u>

Level 13: "Miss Kirby's Room" pp. 66-89.
Objective: To determine word meaning through context clues. (Comprehension)

Now write answers to the following questions about story sentences 1-5.

6. Reread sentence 1 and tell how Jamie helped win the game in the last few minutes.

She helped make the last two outs—first, by tagging the runner at home

plate, and then by throwing Hank out at 1st base.

_____

7. Reread sentence 2 on page 14 and tell in your own words how you think Susan felt

about Jamie's rabbit's foot.

She didn't like it. She thought Jamie should wear a ribbon in her hair

like the other girls.

8. Reread sentence 3 on page 14 and explain why the class was so uncomfortable at

this time in the story.

Miss Kirby had just told them they wouldn't hear _Treasure Island_ again until

the thief returned the dollar.

9. Reread sentence 4. What had just happened to make Susan feel so jealous?

Susan was spending the night at Pam's. Pam had just told Susan how much

she liked Jamie. It was almost "more than Susan could bear."

_____

10. Reread sentence 5. Why do you think the children didn't want to be around Jamie?

By now the rumor had spread that she was the thief.

_____

11. What evidence was there that Jamie was the thief? _____ Susan had seen Jamie

putting a dollar in Nick's cubbyhole.

12. If you had been Susan, would you have thought Jamie was guilty? Why or why not?

What would you have done if you were Susan? _____

Answers will vary and they should help inspire a good discussion before

continuing the story.

_____

Level 13: "Miss Kirby's Room" pp. 66-89.

Objective: To recall details in the selection. (Comprehension)

15

May I Have the Envelope, Please?

Five awards have been chosen for some of the characters in "Miss Kirby's Room." Three characters have been nominated for each award. Your class will elect the winner.

Think about the qualifications of each character and then vote for one. In one or two sentences, explain what this character did to win your vote.

When the votes have been counted, you may wish to enact an awards presentation like the ones we often see on TV. Nominated characters may be seated in the audience. Before each award is announced, nominees may come forward and act out a scene to show why they deserve to win.

---

1. The first award is for the MOST ADMIRABLE CHARACTER in "Miss Kirby's Room."

The nominees are: MISS KIRBY   NICK   JAMIE

I vote for ___Answers may vary___ . This character was especially admirable when

_____

_____ .

---

2. The second award is for the MOST UNADMIRABLE CHARACTER in the story.

The nominees are: SUSAN   THE THIEF   CHRISSIE

I vote for_____. This character was most unadmirable when

_____

_____ .

Level 13: "Miss Kirby's Room" pp. 66-89.

Objective: To describe a given character in terms of explicit and implicit character traits. (Comprehension)

3. The third award is for the ANGRIEST CHARACTER in "Miss Kirby's Room."

The nominees are: NICK   MR. BLAIR   SUSAN

I vote for_____. This character was especially angry when

_____

_____.

4. The fourth award is for the UNHAPPIEST CHARACTER during the story.

The nominees are: NICK   PEE WEE   SUSAN

I vote for_____. This character was especially unhappy when

_____

_____.

5. The fifth award is for the HAPPIEST CHARACTER at the end of the story.

The nominees are: SUSAN   MISS KIRBY   JAMIE

I vote for_____. This character was especially happy when

_____

_____.

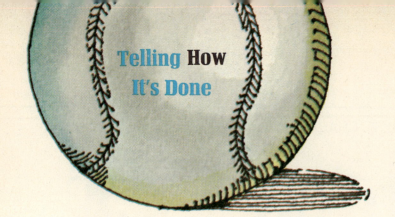

Telling **How** It's Done

The batter swung _____.

Which of the following words might be used to complete this sentence? Underline your answers.

smooth	<u>wildly</u>	<u>powerfully</u>	effortless	awkwardness	mystery
<u>smoothly</u>	wild	powerful	<u>effortlessly</u>	<u>awkwardly</u>	<u>mysteriously</u>

A.

B.

C.

Write in the missing words.

The batter swung **A.** _____powerfully_____ **B.** _____effortlessly_____ **C.** _____awkwardly_____

1. What ending do all of the words that may follow <u>swung</u> share? _____ly_____

2. Each of these words tells us something about _____how_____ the batter swung.

3. Words, such as <u>smoothly</u>, <u>wildly</u>, and <u>powerfully</u>, add meaning to the verb <u>swung</u>.
   Words that **add** meaning to **verbs** are called_____adverbs_____.

4. Adverbs add meaning to verbs just as adjectives add meaning to _____nouns_____.

5. Many adverbs are made from adjectives. What ending must we add to the following adjectives to change them to adverbs? _____ly_____. Write the adverb form of each adjective. Be sure to change <u>y</u> to <u>i</u> before adding <u>-ly</u> to <u>happy</u> and <u>speedy</u>.

ADJECTIVE	ADVERB	ADJECTIVE	ADVERB
suspicious	suspiciously	happy	happily
jealous	jealously	proud	proudly
sad	sadly	kind	kindly
anxious	anxiously	speedy	speedily

18

Level 13: "Miss Kirby's Room" pp. 66-89; "Until I Was Ten" pp. 92-103.

Objectives: To identify adverbs as words that describe verbs. To construct adverbs from adjectives. (Language) To use context clues to determine the meaning of adverbs. (Comprehension)

Now complete the following sentences with each of your new adverbs.

1. Jamie let the ball fly_____speedily_____to first base.

2. After defeating Mrs. Otto's room, Nick walked_____proudly_____off the field.

3. Miss Kirby listened_____kindly_____as Nick told her of the missing dollar.

4. Everyone looked_____suspiciously_____at everyone else after Miss Kirby explained what happened.

5. Pam praised Jamie, and Susan listened_____jealously_____.

6. After the championship game, Pee Wee sat down_____sadly_____and began to cry.

7. The class waited_____anxiously_____to hear *Treasure Island* again.

8. Jamie listened_____happily_____as Miss Kirby began to read her favorite story once more.

Meaning from Context Clues

Here are some adverbs David McCord uses in "Until I Was Ten." Each one has several meanings. How can we know which meaning Mr. McCord wants us to use? To know this, we need to look at the adverb in its sentence context. For example, <u>happily</u> can mean <u>cheerfully</u>, <u>joyfully</u>, or <u>luckily</u>. However, in this sentence—"But today we seem to live for speed alone, as I, happily, did not"—we know that <u>luckily</u> makes the most sense. Find each adverb on its listed page and decide which meaning best fits in the sentence. Underline it.

Page	Adverb	Which definition makes most sense in the sentence?		
1. 93	happily	cheerfully	joyfully	<u>luckily</u>
2. 93	steadily	<u>continuously</u>	evenly	smoothly
3. 95	rarely	excellently	<u>seldom</u>	exceptionally
4. 97	boldly	impolitely	abruptly	<u>fearlessly</u>
5. 102	simply	<u>merely</u>	easily	foolishly
6. 102	nearly	closely	<u>almost</u>	about

Details, Details, Details...

Skim the following paragraphs. As you read, keep in mind how David McCord describes his summers as a young boy. Try to remember the sights, sounds, and experiences he tells about. Then test your memory of these details. Put a check mark in front of each sentence that gives a true detail from the paragraphs.

The roads in every direction were dirt —not paved. We hardly ever saw more than two or three noisy, backfiring automobiles in a day. Often the driver was busy changing a tire. If we didn't own a horse, we rented one. My mother (who had ridden the plains around Denver as a little girl) drove me about the countryside in a high-wheeled cart.

I remember those drives mostly for the strong sea-smell of the marshlands. I remember them for the sight of soaring gulls and the swifter flight of terns as we neared the sea. There were bicycle trips with my parents. We had no boat. But we used to spend hours at the seashore all alone. And on the hard sand, my father and I would fly a big box kite.

BEFORE YOU BEGIN, COVER THE SELECTION ABOVE WITH A SHEET OF PAPER.

_____**1.** The roads in the country were paved in every direction.

✔_____**2.** Automobiles were noisy and not often seen.

_____**3.** People who did not own a horse could rent an automobile.

✔_____**4.** The smell of the sea was strong near the marshlands.

✔_____**5.** Nearing the sea, one could see soaring gulls.

_____**6.** Long bicycle trips ended with picnics at the shore.

_____**7.** Hours were spent sailing lazily in the clear waters.

✔_____**8.** Time would pass while flying a big box kite.

Now uncover the selection above. Check your own answers by rereading the selection.

Score your answers. How many did you check correctly? _____
8:      YOU HAVE A PERFECT SCORE, SHARP EYES.
6-7:   YOU ARE A LITTLE FUZZY.
4-5:   YOU NEED MORE LIGHT ON THE SUBJECT.
0-3:   TRY AGAIN; PRACTICE MAKES PERFECT.

Level 13: "Until I Was Ten" pp. 92-103.

Objective: To recall relevant details after skimming the selection. (Comprehension)

Reading for Main Ideas

Answer the questions below by putting a check in front of the best answer.

1. Read page 92. Then decide which of the following statements best describes the main idea of David McCord's first paragraph.

    _____ a. The reader shouldn't skip any lines of Mr. McCord's poetry.

    ✔ b. Mr. McCord is sharing this part of his life because it was so important to his becoming a poet.

    _____ c. Mr. McCord is going to teach the reader how to become a poet.

2. Read the first paragraph on page 93 beginning, "Of course . . ." Then decide which of these sentences is closest to stating its main idea.

    _____ a. There is rhythm in our world today.

    _____ b. The world of today is crowded and fast paced.

    ✔ c. There was more time to observe and enjoy life when David McCord was a young boy than there is today.

3. Read the paragraph beginning with the sentence, "Several times each year I went up to New York with my mother." This paragraph is mostly about—

    _____ a. the heavy boat traffic in New York Harbor.

    ✔ b. the joy of taking a ferry boat across the river.

    _____ c. the old sailing ships standing in the harbor.

4. Read from page 99, "All this time . . ." to the bottom of page 100, ". . . the right order." Which of these statements best sums up the main idea of this *passage* (portion of the selection)?

    ✔ a. David McCord received the love of language, poetry, and song from several members of his family.

    _____ b. David McCord's mother and grandmother were fine singers.

    _____ c. David McCord's Uncle Robert was full of Japan, books and poems, imagination, and humor.

5. Which of these statements best summarizes the main idea of McCord's entire essay "Until I Was Ten"?

    _____ a. *Red Fox* was the one book that made David want to become a writer.

    _____ b. It is important to be by yourself if you want to be a poet.

    ✔ c. Most of the important events leading Mr. McCord to become a poet occurred in his childhood.

Level 13: "Until I Was Ten" pp. 92-103.

21

Objective: To identify main ideas in a selection. (Comprehension)

David McCord writes in "Until I Was Ten," "From the beginning I was fascinated by the sight and sound and shape of everything that moved with **rhythm**." Mr. McCord has helped us to see that rhythm is everywhere. Poetry, the repetition of words, sounds, and sound patterns all help to provide rhythm. Read each group of words below. One of the items in each group does not follow the rhythmic pattern of the other words. See if you can find it and tell why it doesn't belong.

RHYTHM IS
A PATTERN
REPEATED

1. a. pickety	b. pickety	c. pickety	d. pickle
<u>d</u> because it doesn't repeat the whole word ___pickety___.			
2. a. somehow	b. somehow	c. anyhow	d. somehow
<u>c</u> because the first part of the word is not ___some___.			REPEATING WHOLE WORDS

3. a. lilting	b. wilting	c. languid	d. lizard
<u>b</u> because it begins with the sound of [w] instead of [l].			
4. a. Sarah	b. Cynthia	c. Sylvia	d. Jones
<u>d</u> because it begins with the sound of [j] instead of [s].			REPEATING FIRST SOUNDS: ALLITERATION

5. a. groan	b. growl	c. fowl	d. owl
<u>a</u> because it doesn't rhyme with end sounds in ___owl___.			
6. a. walk/talk	b. words/birds	c. fly/flee	d. bear/where
<u>c</u> because the words don't have the same ___end___ sound.			REPEATING END SOUNDS: RHYME

7. a. batt er y	b. re call	c. sym pho ny	d. tel e phone
<u>b</u> because its stress is ___´ /___ instead of ___/ ` `___.			
8. a. the newt	b. a brute	c. so cute	d. toots a flute
<u>d</u> because it has an ___extra___ long beat.			REPEATING PATTERN OF BEATS: METER

Level 13: "Until I Was Ten" pp. 92-103.

Objective: To identify the major characteristics of rhythm. (Literary Skills)

JUST LIKE...

One way to describe things more vividly is to use comparisons in your writing and speaking. That is, describe something you know well by comparing it to something else. Check the first example below to get the idea. Then think of comparisons that might help tell what is happening in the following sentences.

1. The children burst out of school just like

    twenty-two ____firecrackers____ , zooming _____ , exploding _____ .

2. After the earthquake, the buildings looked just like

    crushed _____ , flattened _____ , a pile of _____ .

3. The children listening to the ghost story huddled together like

    scared _____ , timid _____ , silly _____ .

4. When the cat saw the boy poke her kitten, she acted like

    a raging _____ , a wild _____ , a ferocious _____ .

5. When the firefighter praised the boy, the boy felt like
    a real _____ , a gallant _____ , a brave _____ .

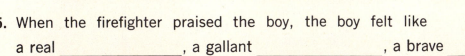

CHECK YOUR MEMORY

Here is a list of the stories in Unit 1. Use the letters next to each title to answer the questions below.

a. "The Magnificent Brain Concocts a Recipe"

b. "Periwinkle Jones"

c. "The Boy Who Changed His Mind"

d. "The Fun They Had"

e. "Miss Kirby's Room"

f. "Until I Was Ten"

Where Did It Happen?

Here are some story settings. Write the letter of the title that goes with each setting.

_c_ **1.** A housing project in a large city in the present.

_b_ **2.** A small Oklahoma town in the present.

_f_ **3.** New York City and Long Island in the early 1900s.

_d_ **4.** A home in the future—2157 A.D.

Who Is the Friend?

On the left is a list of the main characters in the stories. Next to it is a list of their friends. Write the letter of the friend's name on the line next to each main character's name.

1. Margie   _c_   **a.** Shoie

2. Periwinkle   _e_   **b.** Nick

3. Alvin   _a_   **c.** Tommy

4. Jamie   _b_   **d.** Joey

5. Reggie   _d_   **e.** Oscar

Level 13: Unit 1 Review

Objectives: To identify setting, characters, and plot elements. (Comprehension)

What Is It All About?

These phrases describe what the stories are about. Write the letter of the title that goes with each. Turn back to page 24 for the titles.

___d___ **1.** machines and learning

___f___ **2.** poetry and experience

___e___ **3.** baseball and honesty

___a___ **4.** candy and creativity

___c___ **5.** a baby bird and caring

___b___ **6.** a treasure hunt and exaggeration

Another Word That Means the Same Thing

Read the list of words below. Then read the sentences. Find a **synonym** in the list for the underlined word in each sentence. Then write the letter of that synonym in the blank before the sentence. The first one is done for you.

a. fledgling	**d.** nearest	**g.** gingerly	**j.** magnificent
b. determination	**e.** seething	**h.** ducked	
c. pronounced	**f.** amazing	**i.** mistake	

___d___ **1.** Reggie was always closest to the door at the final bell.

___g___ **2.** He held the blue jay gently in his hands.

___i___ **3.** Whoever stole Nick's dollar made an error in judgment.

___b___ **4.** Alvin liked his little sister's spunk.

___h___ **5.** Jamie lowered her head as her face got red.

___f___ **6.** It was surprising what a relief a spelling lesson could be.

___j___ **7.** The children hoped their candy would be fantastic.

___e___ **8.** Periwinkle's imagination was bubbling with ideas.

___c___ **9.** Margie said the word *centuries* carefully.

___a___ **10.** The baby bird could not yet fly.

Suspense, Surprise, and Delight

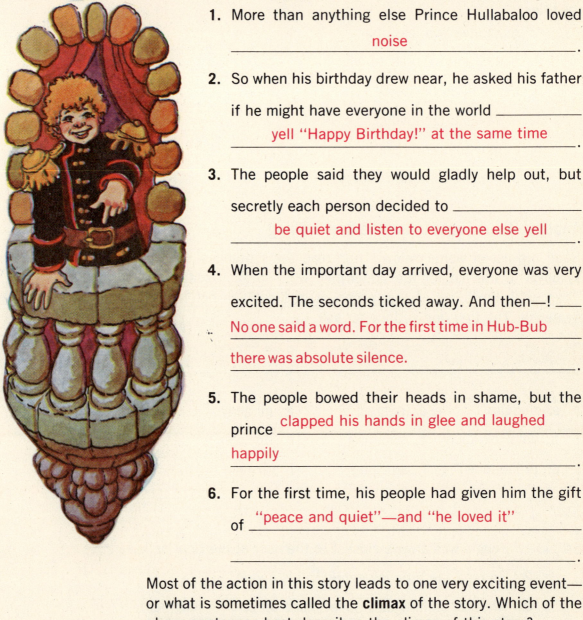

Complete the following sentences in your own words to help retell "The Loudest Noise in the World."

1. More than anything else Prince Hullabaloo loved __noise__.

2. So when his birthday drew near, he asked his father if he might have everyone in the world __yell "Happy Birthday!" at the same time__.

3. The people said they would gladly help out, but secretly each person decided to __be quiet and listen to everyone else yell__.

4. When the important day arrived, everyone was very excited. The seconds ticked away. And then—! __No one said a word. For the first time in Hub-Bub there was absolute silence.__

5. The people bowed their heads in shame, but the prince __clapped his hands in glee and laughed happily__.

6. For the first time, his people had given him the gift of __"peace and quiet"—and "he loved it"__.

Most of the action in this story leads to one very exciting event—or what is sometimes called the **climax** of the story. Which of the above sentences best describes the climax of this story?

Sentence number __4__.

We might say the **climax** helps answer the most important question in the story. Which of the questions below is answered by the climax in "The Loudest Noise in the World"? Put a check in front of the best choice.

_____ a. What did the Prince want everyone to do?

_____ b. How did everyone find out about the Prince's wish?

___✓___ c. What did everyone do when the important moment arrived?

26

Level 13: "The Loudest Noise in the World" pp. 108-117.

Objective: To identify climax in a selection in terms of the development of the plot. (Comprehension)

HOW DO WE SPELL THE SOUND OF ā ?

If you fill the blanks with the right letters, you will have a poem about a white pony.

Neigh

My white pony has a black m a n e .

He likes to gallop in the r a i n .

I would rather ride him than a pl a ne !

I would rather ride him than a tr a i n!

But what do my n eigh bors s ay ,

What do my n eigh bors s ay ,

When my pony says "N eigh , N eigh "?

Why, th ey all go aw ay

    For a very long st ay .

Even that l a dy, dear Mrs. O'Gr a dy

Thinks it a str a i n to rem a i n.

All of the letters you just wrote spell the same long vowel sound. Is this the sound of a in the word ma, mat, or mate?

_____ mate _____

Here are six different spelling patterns for the long vowel sound you hear in **cake**. Write the words from the poem that are spelled with each pattern. The hyphen between a-e stands for any consonant letter.

a-e	ai	ay	ey	eigh	a
mane	rain	say	they	neigh	lady
plane	train	away		neighbors	O'Grady
	strain	stay			
	remain				

Not many English words spell the long vowel sound ā with **ey** or **eigh,** but many English words spell the sound of ā with the letters **a-e** and **ai.** On a separate sheet of paper, write **a-e** and **ai** as two column headings. Then write as many words as you can think of under each spelling pattern.

Level 13: "The Loudest Noise in the World" pp. 108-117.

Objective: To identify these spellings for the vowel sound /ey/ as in *cake: a, a-e, ai, ay, ey, eigh.* (Decoding/Encoding Skills)

WORDS AND THEIR PARTS

See if you can complete each of the word puzzles below.

1. Tall is to taller
   as short is to _____ shorter _____ .

2. Loud is to loudly
   as quiet is to _____ quietly _____ .

3. Delighted is to delight
   as shouted is to _____ shout _____ .

4. Noisiest is to noise
   as slammiest is to _____ slam _____ .

5. Drummer is to drum
   as runner is to _____ run _____ .

6. Prince is to princes
   as _____ visitor _____ is to visitors.

7. Clap is to clapping
   as _____ sing _____ is to singing.

8. Great is to greater and greatest as
   large is to _____ larger _____ and _____ largest _____ .

9. Unhappy is to happy
   as _____ uneven _____ is to even.

10. Preview is to view as
    precaution is to _____ caution _____ .

11. Loud is to super-loud as quiet
    is to _____ super-quiet _____ .

12. Happiness is to happy
    as sadness is to _____ sad _____ .

13. Warmly is to warm
    as friendly is to _____ friend _____ .

14. Unhappily is to happy
    as _____ unfriendly _____ is to friend.

Underline the **base** of each word below.

teacher	honoring	suddenly	meeting	shrillest
undo	sounded	gladness	discover	return

Underline the **affix** in each word below.

assignment	wooded	longer	untrue	nearest
disappear	quickly	preview	dangerous	undone

Level 13: "The Loudest Noise in the World" pp. 108-117.
Objective: To distinguish the base of a word from other word parts. (Language Skills)

Theme and Setting

Read the following story carefully. Then turn the page and answer each question.

A Different Kind of Medicine

Annie lived with her parents and her two brothers in an apartment in a very large city. The landlord said the apartment had three and a half rooms, but if you didn't count the kitchen and the bathroom, there were really only two rooms. It wasn't a bad apartment; it was just too small. Inside, there was no room to play. Outside, there were no trees, no flowers, no grass—only streets, sidewalks, and front steps.

One spring afternoon Annie suddenly had a wonderful idea. She asked her father to help her build a window box so she could grow some flowers. He agreed, and Annie promised to help mop the halls in the building. She didn't like to mop, but when she remembered that she was earning money for her plants, the work was easier. By the end of the month, Annie had two nice geranium plants and a bright green window box.

Annie took good care of her plants. She even talked to them. And by midsummer one of them had lots of beautiful flowers. But the other one drooped sadly.

The droopy plant made Annie unhappy, but the healthy one was so lovely that she felt proud, too. Wherever she went, she looked for other window-box geraniums. She compared them with her own, and none seemed as beautiful or as big.

Then one day, the lady in the apartment next door was rushed to the hospital. Annie's mother said the lady was very lonely. But she was very nice, too, and Annie liked her.

Annie thought about the lady all the next day. That night when she wasn't home at dinner time, her parents began to worry. They called and looked everywhere. Just as they were about to call the police, the door opened and in walked Annie.

The rest of the family all started to talk at once. Where had she been? Why was she so late? What was the matter?

"I went by myself to the hospital," Annie said quietly. "I went to see Mrs. Johnson. She was in a big room with lots and lots of other sick people. I took her my good geranium, and she said it made her feel better right away. I'm glad it made her happy, but now, all I have is a sick geranium. How am I going to make *it* feel better!"

Level 13: "The Boy Who Wouldn't Talk" pp. 118-134.

Objective: To infer the major story theme. To infer the effect of the setting upon plot development in a selection. (Comprehension)

Theme and Setting

The **theme** of a story is its general main idea. The **setting** of a story is the time and place of the action. Complete the following questions about theme and setting. Write the letter of the correct answer in the blank following each question.

1. Which of the following sentences best states the theme of the story "A Different Kind of Medicine?" ___c___
   a. Living in a small, crowded apartment is very lonely and sad.
   b. Things mean a lot more to people if they have to work hard to get them.
   c. A part of being unselfish is doing something to make someone else happy.

2. Where does the story about Annie and her geraniums take place? ___b___
   a. In a small town near a hospital.
   b. In an apartment in a large city.
   c. In a small house with no trees or grass outside.

3. When do you think the story takes place? ___a___
   a. In the spring and summer seasons.
   b. During the winter a long time ago.
   c. On a Saturday in September.

4. Why do you think Annie worked so hard to earn money for a window box to grow some flowers? ___c___
   a. She was bored and didn't have anything else to do.
   b. So that she could give her geraniums away to someone.
   c. To make the outside of her apartment brighter and prettier.

5. Why do you think Mrs. Johnson appreciated the geranium so much? ___b___
   a. Annie had mopped floors to earn money for the flowers.
   b. Being in a hospital room with other sick people can be lonely and depressing.
   c. She was a nice person and liked Annie.

6. Why do you think Annie decided to give away her one healthy geranium plant to Mrs. Johnson? ___a___
   a. Mrs. Johnson went from a dreary apartment building to a dreary hospital and needed something to cheer her up.
   b. Annie did not want to take care of the geranium anymore.
   c. Winter was on its way and the plants would die outside anyway.

Level 13: "The Boy Who Wouldn't Talk" pp. 118-134.

Objective: To infer the major story theme. To infer the effect of the setting upon plot development in a selection. (Comprehension)

Be a Sound Detective
Find the Letters That Spell ē

Each of the words in the box at the left has the long vowel sound you hear in **leaf**. Find and underline the word in each row that does not have that sound. The first one is done for you.

be	she	we	weep	mean	<u>bed</u>
sea	teacher	<u>steak</u>	cream	dream	lean
green	free	street	eel	<u>set</u>	feel
funny	Ricky	Yvonne	<u>yet</u>	happy	gladly

Each of the words below contains the long vowel sound ē . Complete the words by filling in the missing letters. Then write the letter or pair of letters that spell this vowel sound above the words on the blank lines. The first one is completed for you.

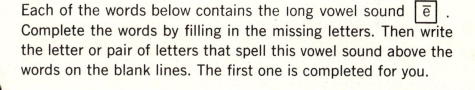

ee	ea	y	e
s ee	p ea ch	Rick y	b e
d ee p	r ea ch	stick y	de cide
f ee l	be a m	happ y	be low
str ee t	te a m	warml y	be gin

Here are some rhymes which end in the sound ē . Read each rhyme and fill in the missing rhyme word. The first is done for you.

Hello, Ricky!

Good-by, ___Nicky___ !

Is it he?

Is it she?

No, it's ___me___ .

Do you see

A little ___tree___ ?

Reach, reach

For a ___peach___ .

Level 13: "The Boy Who Wouldn't Talk" pp. 118-134.

Objective: To identify these spellings for the vowel sound /iy/ as in *leaf: e, ee, ea, y.* (Decoding/Encoding Skills)

31

HOW DO WE SPELL THE SOUND OF ī?

The colored letters in the title of the poem are clues to the missing letters in the poem. Fill in the letters. Then do the exercises to the right.

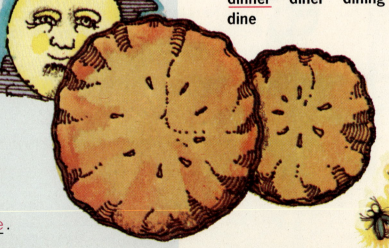

S_i_de by s_i_de
And br_igh_t with l_igh_t
Two firefl_ie_s
Brave the n_igh_t.

They think the moon
Is nectar p_ie_,
And that is wh_y_
They fl_y_ so h_igh_.

Bes_id_es, they l_i_k_e_
The exerc_is_e
And think it w_is_e
To fl_y_ the sk_ie_s
In search of p_ie_s!

Wh_i_l_e_ with del_igh_t
They may rec_it_e
Their venture
Into n_igh_t,

You and _I_
Can only s_igh_,
For we can't fl_y_
Into the sk_y_
To look for nectar p_ie_.

Why I Sigh for Pie!

1. Which of the following words has the vowel sound you hear in **kite** or ī : **may, my, mit?**

   _my_

2. Which of the following letters or letter groups does <u>not</u> spell the long vowel sound ī in the poem:

   i-e, y, igh, i, ai, ie?

   _ai_

3. Write a rhyming word from the poem for each of the words below:

   light   why   skies   wide

   night   fly   pies   side

4. Underline the words that do <u>not</u> have the long vowel sound ī in the lines below.

   by   why   <u>silly</u>   try
   sigh   <u>sit</u>   sight   site
   tie   die   lie   <u>chief</u>
   like   <u>lick</u>   life   line
   <u>dinner</u>   diner   dining
   dine

Level 13: "What Is Your Name?" pp. 135-137.

Objective: To identify these spellings for the vowel sound /ay/ as in *kite: i, i-e, y, igh, ie.* (Decoding/Encoding Skills)

NAME GAME

Many names rhyme with other names. In the following box there are ten pairs of rhyming first names. See if you can find each pair. Write the names on the lines below.

Carrie	Jim	Donald	Bill	Lee	Fay	Fran
Jane	Randy	Dan	Elaine	Doris	Bea	Jill
Kim	Ronald	Morris	Sandy	Larry	Kay	

Carrie	Jane	Kim	Dan	Morris
Larry	Elaine	Jim	Fran	Doris

Fay	Randy	Donald	Bill	Bea
Kay	Sandy	Ronald	Jill	Lee

1. Do rhyming words have the same **beginning** or **end** sounds?   end

2. Are the parts of words that **sound alike** always **spelled alike**?   No

3. Which four of these names have the vowel sound you hear in **day**?

Jane	Elaine	Fay	Kay

HEBREW

Ann = grace
Judith = praised
Ruth = friend
David = beloved

GREEK

Agnes = gentle
Alice = truth
Philip = loves
       horses
Stephen = crown

LATIN

Patrick = patrician
Paul = little
Victor = conqueror
Amy = beloved

What's in a Name?

To what names in the column are these names related?

GIVEN NAME		SURNAME	
1. Patricia	Patrick	4. Paulson	Paul
2. Paula	Paul	5. Davidson	David
3. Victoria	Victor	6. Stephenson	Stephen

Using information from the column, choose a good name to fit these descriptions.

1. a graceful girl   Ann
2. a boy who loves horses   Philip
3. a much praised girl   Judith
4. a girl with many friends   Ruth

Objective: To identify and supply words that share the same end sounds. (Decoding/Encoding Skills)

SUBJECT PRONOUN & SUBJECT PHRASES

A subject pronoun may stand for a single noun subject or an entire noun phrase.

Tom dreamed.   *A short and unexpected adventure* ended.

He dreamed.   *It* ended.

Underline the **subject noun phrase** in each of the following sentences. Then write a **pronoun** that may be used in its place.

1. The noisy city of Hub-Bub was well-known.

   It

2. Two cows and a bull are grazing.

   They

3. Miss Kirby was our teacher.

   She

4. His younger brother forgot the hamster.

   He

5. The umbrella came in handy when the rain began.

   It

6. The young girl hit a home run.

   She

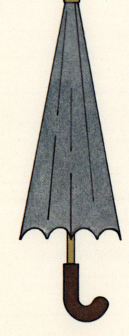

The pronouns in these sentences stand for nouns from some of the stories you've read. Write the **noun phrase** each **pronoun** stands for.

1. **They** concocted a magnificent mess in the kitchen. ____Alvin, Shoie, and Daphne____

2. **We** were very bored until Periwinkle arrived. ____Oscar and Sam____

3. **She** read Treasure Island to her class. ____Miss Kirby____

4. **I** did not want to talk. ____Carlos____

5. **You** know all about us if you've read this far in your book. ____Pupil's name____

    Level 13: "What Is Your Name?" pp. 135-137.

Objective: To use pronouns in place of noun phrases in a subject noun phrase. (Language Skills)

Getting the Message

Read the following story and answer the questions that follow.

Once upon a time there were three brothers. When they were grown, their father—who was a successful farmer—said, "I will give you a large part of my land. You may decide together what you will do with it."

The brothers decided they, too, would like to become successful farmers. But first they would build themselves a comfortable house. Their land was located just off a windy seacoast. Yet they chose to build their first house out of straw. They thought a straw house would be both quick and inexpensive to build. Before they had finished building their house, a strong wind came up and scattered the house all over the countryside.

The brothers decided to try again. But this time they used sticks they had gathered from a nearby woods. They hoped to build a stronger house. Almost as soon as their second house was finished, a furious storm came up. It blew the house to the ground.

Once again the brothers talked it over. This time they decided to go to town, buy bricks and cement, and build a much stronger house. After several weeks of living in their new house, a mighty hurricane hurled itself across the land. When the winds reached the brothers' house,—!

1. Suppose this story had a plot (story action) with a series of repeated events like the story "Talk." What would probably happen to the brothers' third house? _____
   <u>The house would be destroyed by the hurricane.</u>

2. Why, in this particular story, might it make sense for the third house to stand up against a mighty hurricane? <u>It is built of much stronger</u>
   <u>materials than the first two houses. The brothers may</u>
   <u>have learned a lesson.</u>

3. What familiar nursery tale has a plot similar to this story? _____
   <u>"The Three Little Pigs"</u>

4. What happened to the brick house in that story?
   <u>It remained standing even after the wolf huffed and puffed.</u>

5. Put a check in front of the statement below that best summarizes the *theme* or lesson to be learned from the story of the three brothers.

   _____ a. One building material is just about as good as another.

   ✔ _____ b. If you live where there are strong winds, build a house with strong materials.

   _____ c. When it comes to building a house, three heads are better than one.

Objective: To predict what may happen next in a selection. To infer the theme in a selection when it is not specifically/explicitly stated. (Comprehension)

TALK ABOUT "TALK"

A. Write the letter of the words in the right-hand column by the words they best describe in the left-hand column.

___d___ **1.** fantastic   **a.** a lesson about life

___c___ **2.** refrain   **b.** the time and place

___b___ **3.** setting   **c.** repeated words and sentences

___a___ **4.** moral   **d.** wild, unreal

B. Underline one of the two blue words in each of the following sentences to make the sentence true. Then underline the words on the right that give evidence from the story.

"Talk" as a Folktale	Evidence from the Story
1. "Talk" is a folktale with many factual/<u>fantastic</u> events.	<u>talking yam</u> cow chewing cud weaver with cloth <u>talking stool</u>
2. "Talk" is a folktale that takes place in modern times/<u>long ago</u>.	talking by telephone <u>traveling on foot</u> <u>the first word in the story</u> the last word in the story
3. "Talk" takes place in a warm <u>African country near water</u>/cold Asian country near mountains.	stones <u>palm trees</u> dogs <u>Gulf of Guinea</u> sheep villages
4. Like most folktales, "Talk" has a number of rhymes/<u>refrains</u>.	"Why's the hurry?" <u>"Leave me alone."</u> "Put that branch down!" The chief sat on his stool.
5. "Talk" also like some folktales has a moral/<u>puzzling</u> ending.	Be kind to yams. <u>Take other people's complaints</u> <u>seriously.</u> Live in the city.

C. Answer the following questions on a separate sheet of paper.

1. Did the people the farmer met believe his story
    a. as soon as they heard it?
    b. after they thought about it awhile?
    c. after something similar happened to them? (X)

2. What is the difference in the story between the way the people act when they hear about the farmer's experience and when it happens to them?

3. What do you think the chief did after his stool talked to him? Why do you think so?

Objective: To identify a folktale by describing its major characteristics. (Literary Skills)

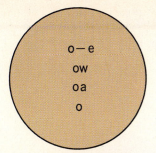

How Do We Spell the Sound of $\bar{o}$?

o — e
ow
oa
o

There are four common ways to spell the long vowel sound you hear in **goat**. Find out all four ways by filling in the letter or word missing in the poem below. Then read the entire poem to yourself from beginning to end.

Like other English vowel sounds that we know,

Here are four ways to spell the sound of $\bar{o}$.

The first common spelling has letters three:

An **o**, a **consonant,** and a **silent** ___e___ .

A second spelling that just might trouble you—

The long vowel $\bar{o}$ with **o** and ___w___ .

You may also not guess or be able to say

That some words spell $\bar{o}$ with **o** and ___a___ .

But the simplest spelling in this rhyming game

Spells $\bar{o}$ with the letter that says its ___name___ .

In each of the following word groups, one word does not have the long vowel sound $\bar{o}$. Find the word that does not belong and draw a line through it. Then underline the letters in the remaining words that spell the sound of $\bar{o}$.

Which one doesn't belong?

1.	dr<u>o</u>ne	dr<u>o</u>ve	~~done~~	d<u>o</u>me	d<u>o</u>te
2.	hell<u>o</u>	radi<u>o</u>	b<u>o</u>th	~~got~~	g<u>o</u>
3.	sh<u>ow</u>	~~cow~~	gr<u>ow</u>	fl<u>ow</u>	l<u>ow</u>
4.	c<u>oa</u>ch	g<u>oa</u>l	r<u>oa</u>st	l<u>oa</u>n	~~broad~~

Each of the five words below is spelled with a less common spelling for $\bar{o}$. Underline the letters in each word that stand for $\bar{o}$. Then write these letters above the sample words.

Less frequent spellings for $\bar{o}$

ough	oe	ew	ou	oh
th<u>ough</u>	h<u>oe</u>	s<u>ew</u>	s<u>ou</u>l	<u>oh</u>

Level 13: "Talk," pp. 140-145.

Objective: To identify these spellings for the vowel sound /ow/ as in *goat: o, o-e, oa, ow.* (Decoding/Encoding Skills)

37

comparing word definitions

Each of the words at the left is listed in the Glossary of *Time to Wonder*. Find the word and read its definition. Then decide which of the three blue words at the right has something in common with the Glossary word. Underline your answer and complete the sentence with a word from the Glossary definition.

1. **Dappled** has something in common with leopard—zebra—polar bear

   because both dappled and leopard have the word "spotted" in their definitions.

2. **Cactus** might be compared with cow—porcupine—elephant

   because both words name things that have sharp _____ spines _____ .

3. **Bagpipe** might be compared with drum—violin—organ

   because both words name instruments that make music by pushing air through

   _____ pipes _____ .

4. **Bulldozer** might be compared with shovel—lawn mower—watering can

   because both words name pieces of equipment used to move _____ earth _____ .

5. **Century** might be compared with quarter—half dollar—dollar

   because both words are defined as having a _____ hundred _____ parts.

6. **Feud** might be compared with agreement—argument—agriculture

   because both words represent different stages in a _____ quarrel _____ .

Level 13: "Radio," "The Queen Who Couldn't Make Spice Nuts" pp. 147-156.
Objective: To explore the semantic relationship of selected story words. (Comprehension)

7. **Globe** might be compared with

    triangle—square—<u>sphere</u>

    because both words name things that are shaped like a _____ball_____.

8. **Cinnamon** might be compared with

    <u>nutmeg</u>—meat—porridge

    because both words name a _____spice_____.

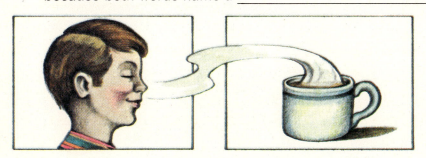

9. **Invisible** has something in common with

    rain—lightning—<u>wind</u>

    because both words are related to things that can't be _____seen_____.

10. **Fragile** has something in common with

    wood—water—<u>glass</u>

    because both words are related to things easily _____broken_____.

11. **Amazement** is related to

    happiness—boredom—<u>awe</u>

    because both words describe a feeling of _____wonder_____.

12. **Solitude** might be compared with

    <u>one</u>—a couple—a crowd

    because both words are related to being _____alone_____.

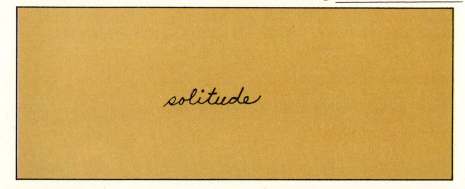

solitude

WORDS ABOUT WORDS

A. Write the letter of the word in Row 2 in front of its **antonym** in Row 1.

ROW 1. _c_ perfect _a_ fortunate _d_ tireless _b_ stand firm

ROW 2. **a.** unfortunate **b.** back down **c.** imperfect **d.** fatigued

B. Write the letter of the word or words in the yellow box beside the story word or words that are **synonyms** in the blue box.

_e_ enchanted _c_ vow _f_ wheeze pipe _a_ absurd

_g_ reconsidered _b_ bridge _h_ chuckling _d_ realizing

a. preposterous   **b.** connect   **c.** promise   **d.** understanding

e. delighted   **f.** harmonica   **g.** thought over   **h.** laughing

C. Write in the missing word in the following two sentences.

1. Words that are **close** in meaning are called _____ synonyms _____.

2. Words that are **opposite** in meaning are called _____ antonyms _____.

D. Each of the following quotations from the selection is followed by two sentences. Circle the letter of the sentence that comes closest to saying what the character really meant.

1. " . . . your own medicine doesn't taste so good . . ."

   a. Those pills of yours have an unpleasant flavor.

   (b.) When you have to do the same thing you've asked others to do, it may not be much fun.

2. " . . . But it's absurd. Preposterous! Ridiculous! How dare she?"

   a. It's amusing! Funny! Hilarious! What a sense of humor!

   (b.) It's amazing! Unbelievable! Absolutely crazy! She's got a lot of nerve!

3. "A really well-rounded king ought to . . ."

   (a.) A king with knowledge about a lot of things should . . .

   b. A full-bodied king should . . .

Level 13: "Radio," "The Queen Who Couldn't Make Spice Nuts" pp. 147-156.

Objectives: To identify antonyms as words with opposite meanings. To identify synonyms as words with similar meanings.
(Language Skills)

From A to Z

Lengthwise began life in the dictionary and ate his way word by word from A to Z. Here are some of Lengthwise's phrases from the story. Although his words usually begin with the same letter, he did not always say them in quite the same order as he swallowed them. Write "the same" next to those words that are in the order Lengthwise ate them. Write the words that are not in **alphabetical** order as they would be arranged in a dictionary or glossary. The first two are done for you.

Remember, when words share the same first letter, alphabetize by their second letters: warm comes before worm.

When words share the first and second letters, alphabetize by their third letters: crispy comes before crunchy.

Words from Lengthwise

As He Said Them	As He Swallowed Them
1. An accurate assumption!	accurate an assumption
2. Aye, aye, absolutely awful!	absolutely awful aye, aye
3. Amazing adventures await.	adventures amazing await
4. Beautiful, big, black beetle	beautiful beetle big black
5. Behold a backward bookworm.	backward behold bookworm
6. Baffled by bewildering bug-babble	baffled bewildering bug-babble by
7. Befriend bewildered bookworm.	the same
8. Bye-bye, boy.	boy bye-bye
9. Zounds! I've lost my zest!	I've lost my zest zounds
10. My zip has come unzippered!	come has my unzippered zip

Level 13: "The Story of Lengthwise" pp. 157-166.

Objective: To relate letter positions in the alphabet to the order of entry words in the dictionary. (Study Skills)

41

Distinctive Dishes in the Dictionary Diet

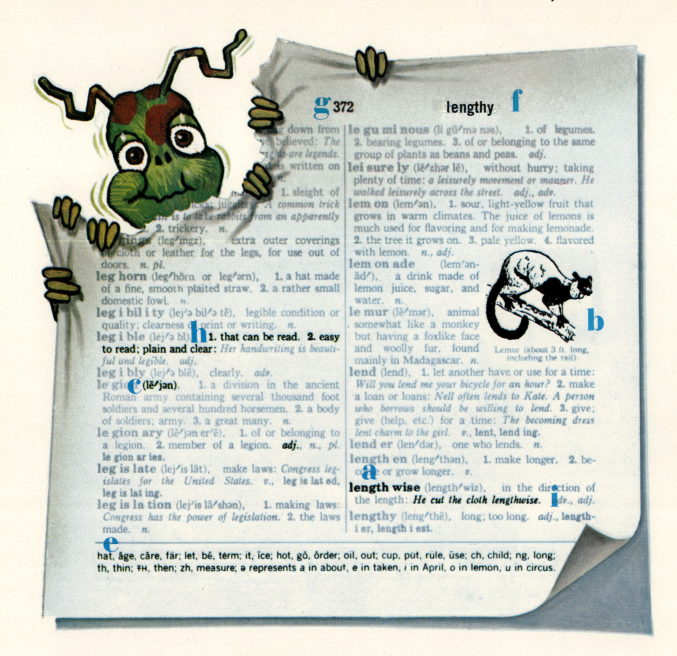

g 372   lengthy **f**

le gu mi nous (li gū′mə nəs),   1. of legumes.
2. bearing legumes. 3. of or belonging to the same
group of plants as beans and peas.   *adj.*

lei sure ly (lē′zhər lē),   without hurry; taking
plenty of time: *a leisurely movement or manner. He
walked leisurely across the street.   adj., adv.*

lem on (lem′ən).   1. sour, light-yellow fruit that
grows in warm climates. The juice of lemons is
much used for flavoring and for making lemonade.
2. the tree it grows on. 3. pale yellow. 4. flavored
with lemon.   *n., adj.*

lem on ade   (lem′ən-
ād′),   a drink made of
lemon juice, sugar, and
water.   *n.*

le mur (lē′mər),   animal
somewhat like a monkey
but having a foxlike face
and woolly fur, found
mainly in Madagascar.   *n.* **b**

Lemur (about 3 ft. long,
including the tail)

...g down from
...believed: *The
...s are legends.*
...written on

...1. sleight of
...juggler; *A common trick
...is to take rabbits from an apparently*
...2. trickery.   *n.*

...kings (leg′ingz),   extra outer coverings
of cloth or leather for the legs, for use out of
doors.   *n. pl.*

leg horn (leg′hôrn or leg′ərn),   1. a hat made
of a fine, smooth plaited straw. 2. a rather small
domestic fowl.   *n.*

leg i bil i ty (lej′ə bil′ə tē),   legible condition or
quality; clearness of print or writing.   *n.*

leg i ble (lej′ə bl) **h** 1. that can be read. 2. easy
to read; plain and clear: *Her handwriting is beautiful and legible.   adj.*

leg i bly (lej′ə blē),   clearly.   *adv.*

le gion **c** (lē′jən)   1. a division in the ancient
Roman army containing several thousand foot
soldiers and several hundred horsemen. 2. a body
of soldiers; army. 3. a great many.   *n.*

le gion ary (lē′jən er′ē),   1. of or belonging to
a legion. 2. member of a legion.   *adj., n., pl.*
le gion ar ies.

leg is late (lej′is lāt),   make laws: *Congress leg-
islates for the United States.   v.,* leg is lat ed,
leg is lat ing.

leg is la tion (lej′is lā′shən),   1. making laws:
Congress has the power of legislation. 2. the laws
made.   *n.*

lend (lend),   1. let another have or use for a time:
Will you lend me your bicycle for an hour? 2. make
a loan or loans: *Nell often lends to Kate. A person
who borrows should be willing to lend.* 3. give;
give (help, etc.) for a time: *The becoming dress
lent charm to the girl.   v.,* lent, lend ing.

lend er (len′dər),   one who lends.   *n.*

length en (leng′thən),   1. make longer. 2. be- **a**
come or grow longer.   *v.*

length wise (length′wīz),   in the direction of
the length: *He cut the cloth lengthwise.* **i** *adv., adj.*

lengthy (leng′thē),   long; too long.   *adj.,* length-
i er, length i est.

e
hat, āge, cāre, fär; let, bē, tėrm; it, īce; hot, gō, ôrder; oil, out; cup, pùt, rüle, ūse; ch, child; ng, long;
th, thin; ⱨ, then; zh, measure; ə represents a in about, e in taken, i in April, o in lemon, u in circus.

Here are some of the different dictionary delicacies that
Lengthwise ate in the course of his unusual diet. See if you
can match the letters above with the terms below in order to
identify each distinctive dictionary dish.

guide words	f	pronunciation respelling	c
illustration	b	sample sentence	i
page number	g	numbered definitions	h
entry word	a	shortened Pronunciation Key	e

Level 13: "The Story of Lengthwise" pp. 157-166.

Objective: To describe the content of a dictionary page and identify its common features. To describe the sequence
of a dictionary entry. (Study Skills)

WHAT HAPPENED WHEN?

The events in a story like the events in real life occur in a certain **order.** Listed below are some of the main events from the life of Thomas Gallaudet (gal ə det′). But they are not arranged in the correct time order. Briefly review "No Schools for the Deaf Ones" on pages 168-175. Then number the events so they are in the same order as they took place in the story.

__4__ **a.** For the first time Alice understood that things had names and could be written.

__7__ **b.** Thomas decided he would help Alice and the other deaf ones who had no schools in America.

__1__ **c.** Thomas Gallaudet wondered what he would do after his graduation from college.

__5__ **d.** Alice showed her father that she understood her first written word.

__8__ **e.** Thomas began teaching Alice, and after college he founded the first school for the deaf in America.

__2__ **f.** One afternoon Thomas saw Alice Cogswell and learned she was deaf and mute.

__6__ **g.** Dr. Cogswell was overjoyed and asked Thomas to teach Alice more written words.

__3__ **h.** Thomas showed Alice his hat and wrote the letters H-A-T in the sand.

Is It True or False?
Check each statement that is true.

_____ **1.** Alice had never been able to speak or hear.

_√_ **2.** The first word Alice learned was *hat.*

_√_ **3.** Thomas helped start the first American school for the deaf.

_____ **4.** Dr. Cogswell sent Alice to England to a special school.

_√_ **5.** Alice spelled with her fingers and used hand signs for different words.

Level 13: "No Schools for the Deaf Ones" pp. 168-175.

Objective: To order events of a story in correct sequence. (Comprehension)

43

"A symbol is anything
that is agreed to stand for something else."

People are the only living things who can invent new symbols and change the meaning of old ones. When many people could not read, picture signs or symbols were hung in front of places of business. These signs helped people know where the businesses were and what could be purchased there. Here are some early signs that stood for the names of old English inns and restaurants. Match the names with each pictured symbol.

1. The Red Coach Inn __b__   **2.** The Three Crowns Inn __a__

3. The Gold Stag Tavern __c__   **4.** The Lion's Head House __d__

In the early 1900s, American businesses often had picture signs to show the kind of store or shop that was inside. Match the following signs with the people listed below.

1. locksmith __d__   2. shoemaker __a__   3. druggist __c__   4. dentist __b__

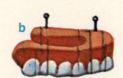
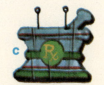

Here are some common signs and symbols used today. Match each sign with the meaning listed below.

1. Mathematics: equals __e__   **2.** Music: quarter rest __d__   **3.** Skull and Crossbones:

4. Olympic Games: __b__   **5.** Money: dollar sign __a__   poison __c__

a.   b.    c.   d.   e.

Level 13: "No Schools for the Deaf Ones" pp. 168-175.

Objectives: To recognize a symbol as a sign that stands for an idea. To identify the thing a symbol represents. (Comprehension)

HOW DO WE SPELL THE SOUNDS OF yü AND ü ?

The long vowel sounds you hear in **moon** and **music** share many of the same spellings. See if you can discover five of the most common spellings by writing in the letters that complete the following words. After writing the missing letters, write the letters that stand for yü or ü in the boxes at right.

hum a tune___	for strumming, a uke___	a kind of feather, a plume___	u–e
a sky color, blue___	not false, but true___	a girl's name, Sue___	ue
a song is music___	a student is a pupil___	like a trumpet, a bugle___	u
not soup, but stew___	not many, but few___	not old, but new___	ew
"magnificent and mellow", the moon___	not warm, but cool___	for sweeping, a broom___	oo

The following spellings are found only in a small number of English words. See if you can write in the missing letters from the clues in the boxes.

ou	wo	ough	o	ui
not me, but you___	not one, but two___	not around, but through___	not did, but do___	not vegetable, but fruit___

iew	eu	eau	ioux
a sight, or a view___	a detective, or a sleuth___	lovely, or beautiful___	an Indian tribe, the Sioux___

Level 13: "No School for the Deaf Ones" pp. 168-175.

Objectives: To identify spellings for the vowel sounds /uw/ as in *moon: oo, ew, ue, ui*; and /yuw/ as in *unicorn: u, u-e, ew*. (Decoding/Encoding Skills)

FINDING THE FACTS

Two of the nonfiction selections in Unit 2 that give factual information are "TEACHER: Anne Sullivan" and "CAREERS: School for Deaf Ones." Briefly skim each selection and then complete the following exercises.

"TEACHER: Anne Sullivan" page 167

The following sentences tell some of the main events in Anne Sullivan's life, but the sentences are out of order. Number them in the order they happened, or in chronological order.

___3___ She graduated first in her class.

___4___ Helen Keller became her pupil.

___2___ She went to the Perkins Institution for the Blind.

___5___ Anne Sullivan helped teach Helen Keller to understand and use language.

___1___ Anne Sullivan was orphaned.

___6___ Helen Keller became famous and gave hope to others with handicaps.

CAREERS: "School for Deaf Ones" pages 176-177

Use the following words from the Career selection to complete these sentences.

sign language	reading lips	hearing aid
microphone	hearing	

1. A device that can be used to help improve some deaf people's hearing is a ___hearing aid___.

2. Deaf people can learn to communicate with their hands by using ___sign language___.

3. An audiologist tests people's ___hearing___.

4. Some deaf people can understand what others are saying by ___reading lips___.

5. Speech teachers may make their voices louder for deaf pupils by speaking into a ___microphone___.

Level 13: "Careers: School for Deaf Ones" pp. 176-177.
Objective: To recall significant details from a selection. (Comprehension)

CHECK YOUR MEMORY

What Kind of Writing Is It?

Below are titles from some of the stories in Unit 2. Above them are the names of different kinds of writing. Match each title with the word that tells what kind of writing it represents.

a. folktale   **b.** poem   **c.** story   **d.** essay   **e.** biography

1. "The Boy Who Wouldn't Talk"   story

2. "What Is Your Name?   essay

3. "Talk"   folktale

4. "Ululation"   poem

5. "No Schools for the Deaf Ones"   biography

Where Did It Happen?

After each setting listed below, write the title of the story.

1. Hartford, Connecticut, in the early 1800s: _____
"No Schools for the Deaf Ones"

2. Modern-day city: _____ "The Boy Who Wouldn't Talk"

3. A dictionary and an imaginary garden: _____ "The Story of Lengthwise"

4. The imaginary kingdom of Hub-Bub: _____ "The Loudest Noise in the World"

5. A country area in Ghana, Africa: _____ "Talk"

Alliteration

Some of these sentences are examples of alliteration or repetition of consonant sounds. Decide which ones they are and put a check mark in the blank before those items. Then underline the repeated beginning consonant letters that spell the sounds that create the alliteration.

✓ **1.** Crunchy, crispy crackers create crumbs in cradles.

___ **2.** A beautiful creature danced evenly forever.

✓ **3.** Munching merrily on maple sugar, Mary mumbled my message.

✓ **4.** Seven southern sisters sat silently for six seconds.

___ **5.** My niece opened presents.

Objectives: To identify genre and setting in selections from Unit 2. (Comprehension/Literary Skills) To identify examples of alliteration. (Language Skills)

THREE WAYS TO SAY NO

You've learned about three ways to give a sentence an opposite meaning in this Unit. Let's see how well you remember them.

1. Words that have opposite meanings are called __antonyms__ .

   Match the words in Column A with their antonyms in Column B.

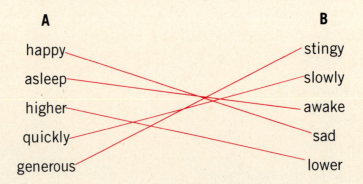

A	B
happy	stingy
asleep	slowly
higher	awake
quickly	sad
generous	lower

2. Negative prefixes also give words opposite meaning. Add the negative prefixes un-, non-, in-, im-, or dis- to these words. Then use the words in sentences.

   __un__likely __im__possible __dis__appear __non__sense __in__correct

   Answers will vary.

   a. _____

   b. _____

   c. _____

   d. _____

   e. _____

3. Another way to give a sentence an opposite meaning is to use a form of the word "do" plus "not."

   Estrellita married Feodor. Estrellita **did not** marry Feodor.

Make these sentences have opposite meanings by using forms of "do" plus "not."

a. Our names rhyme. __Our names do not rhyme.__

b. Most stools speak quietly. __Most stools do not speak quietly.__

   _____

c. He has two radios. __He does not have two radios.__

d. Bookworms eat dictionaries. __Bookworms do not eat dictionaries.__

   _____

Level 13: Unit 2 Review.

Objectives: To identify antonyms. To construct antonyms using negative prefixes. To construct negative sentences. (Language Skills)

WORD MEANING

Over a period of time, most words tend to acquire a number of slightly different meanings. Five words from "James Henry Trotter and the Fantastic Peach" are listed in the exercise below. Each word is followed by two definitions and two sentences. Read each sentence. Then write the number of the definition that tells the meaning of the word as it is used in the sentence.

SEE

1. to perceive, view with the eyes
2. to understand, realize, have mental insight

_1_ **a.** I <u>see</u> the peach.

_2_ **b.** I <u>see</u> what you mean.

BLIND

1. to be unable to view with the eyes
2. to be unable to understand

_2_ **a.** At first Carlos was <u>blind</u> to the fact that Ricky could play make-believe as well as Carlos could.

_1_ **b.** Because Ricky was <u>blind</u>, he enjoyed the flowers by smelling and touching them.

GLOOMY

1. dark or dim, deeply shaded
2. hopeless or sad, pessimistic

_2_ **a.** The Earthworm's <u>gloomy</u> words depressed everyone.

_1_ **b.** The peach's tunnel was fragrant, delicious, and <u>gloomy</u>.

VAIN

1. having too much pride in one's looks
2. without success, useless, empty

_1_ **a.** The Centipede was too <u>vain</u> to go outside without his boots on.

_2_ **b.** James tried in <u>vain</u> to cheer up the Earthworm.

GREAT

1. big; large
2. remarkable

_2_ **a.** The peach tunnel was <u>great</u>.

_1_ **b.** The whale is a <u>great</u> animal.

Level 13: "James Henry Trotter and the Fantastic Peach" pp. 182-205.

Objective: To recognize the multiple meanings of words. (Comprehension)

49

8 Character Sketches

Here are eight sketches of familiar characters in "James Henry Trotter and the Fantastic Peach." Each sketch is accompanied by a descriptive word clue. First, name the characters. Then find a synonym from the bottom of these two pages to match each descriptive adjective.

NAME	Old-Green-Grasshopper	Ladybug
CLUE	polite	friendly
SYNONYM	proper	kindly

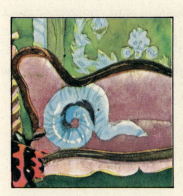

NAME	Earthworm	Centipede
CLUE	pessimistic	proud
SYNONYM	gloomy	vain

SYNONYMS

talented	delicious	intelligent	kindly

Level 13: "James Henry Trotter and the Fantastic Peach" pp. 182-205.

Objective: To identify the characters in a selection. (Comprehension) To use synonyms to determine the meanings of words. (Comprehension)

James   Earthworm   Spider   Ladybug

Centipede   Old-Green-Grasshopper   Silkworm   The Fantastic Peach

Spider	Silkworm	**NAME**
skillful	sleepy	**CLUE**
talented	drowsy	**SYNONYM**

James	The Fantastic Peach	**NAME**
clever	scrumptious	**CLUE**
intelligent	delicious	**SYNONYM**

SYNONYMS

vain   proper   gloomy   drowsy

FACTS ABOUT A FOLKTALE

Draw a line through the word or words in each of the following sentences that is incorrect. Write words to make each sentence correct.

FOLKTALE

1. "Señor Billy Goat" may be described as a folktale because it is make-believe, takes place long ago, teaches a lesson, and is about ~~wealthy and powerful~~ people.   poor, common

SETTING

2. The story takes place in ~~a city~~ in Puerto Rico.   the countryside

CHARACTERS

3. The characters in the story are María, ~~Ricardo,~~ Señor Billy Goat, and la Hormiguita.   Ramón

4. Here are some words that describe the characters.

   a. the husband and wife: old, happy, ~~rich,~~ kind.   poor

   b. Señor Billy Goat: young, ~~weak,~~ selfish.   strong

   c. La Hormiguita: clever, helpful, ~~large.~~   small

PLOT

5. The couple's problem in the folktale is that the billy goat is eating up their ~~orchard.~~   vegetable garden

6. La Hormiguita gets rid of the billy goat by making him think he has stepped into ~~a trap.~~   an ant hill

LESSON

7. This folktale suggests that the weak can overcome the powerful if they use their ~~muscles.~~   brains

FANTASY & REALITY

8. Some of the things that are realistic (could happen) in the story are: people growing gardens and ants ~~talking.~~   walking, stinging, etc.

9. Some of the things that are fantasy (could not happen) are: ants ~~stinging~~ and billy goats talking.   talking, etc.

MOOD

10. "Señor Billy Goat" is a light-hearted and ~~sad~~ story.   happy, funny, etc.

52

Which Word? Which Meaning?

Each of the words listed below has at least two different definitions. Use one of these words to complete each of the sentences that follow. Write the number of the appropriate definition in front of the sentence.

brewing	choice	cry	horns
1. making a boiling drink	**1.** a selection	**1.** to shed tears	**1.** pointed growths on an animal's head
2. to plot, plan	**2.** the best part	**2.** to call loudly	**2.** musical instruments

might	palm	patch	till
1. maybe	**1.** a tree	**1.** piece of ground	**1.** until
2. strength	**2.** part of hand	**2.** to mend	**2.** to plow land

__1__ **1.** The children couldn't wait ____till____ the mail carrier came.

__1__ **2.** Señor Billy Goat tried to butt Maria with his ____horns____.

__2__ **3.** I got a blister on my ____palm____ from carrying the suitcase.

__1__ **4.** Mrs. Wiggs was famous for her cabbage ____patch____.

__2__ **5.** Alvin is ____brewing____ up plans for a surprise party.

__1__ **6.** The weather forecaster said it ____might____ rain today.

__2__ **7.** The woman tried to ____cry____ out for the bus to stop.

__1__ **8.** The customer studied the goods carefully before making a ____choice____.

Now write a sentence for each of the following words using the numbered definition.

brewing 1 **1.** Answers will vary. _____

choice 2 **2.** _____

horns 1 **3.** _____

might 2 **4.** _____

patch 1 **5.** _____

palm 1 **6.** _____

cry 1 **7.** _____

Objective: To use context clues to determine the correct dictionary definition for a given word. (Comprehension)

Books for Information

Answer the following questions with **A (atlas)**, **D (dictionary)**, or **E (encyclopedia)**. Some answers may need more than one letter.

Where would you look to find:

1. the pronunciation of *chaos* ___D___

2. maps of Europe ___A___

3. what countries lie on the equator ___A___

4. if *burro* is a Spanish word ___D___

5. the population of Brazil ___E___

6. the capital of Australia ___A,E___

7. the spelling for *parallel* ___D___

8. the distance between Boston and St. Louis ___A___

9. holidays celebrated in China ___E___

10. how glue is made ___E___

11. the meaning of *collapse* ___D___

12. when George Washington died ___E___

Open your book to the folktale "Señor Billy Goat." Skim each of the pages listed below. Then answer the following questions.

1. Page 207: What clues are we given that suggest María and Ramón aren't lazy people who sleep into the afternoon? ___"In the morning . . ."___ ___". . . busy brewing coffee . . ."___

2. Page 207: What do María and Ramón do after they finish "arguing" about their favorite crops that tells us they aren't serious? ___They laugh and turn to enjoy their coffee.___

3. Page 208: What words does Ramón use with Señor Billy Goat that suggest he is a polite person? ___Buenos días, please___

4. Page 209: What do Ramón and María do after being chased by the billy goat that shows how unhappy they feel? ___Cry___

5. Page 209: What clue tells us that la Hormiguita is a quiet, soft-spoken creature? ___She whispered softly.___

Level 13: "Señor Billy Goat" pp. 206-211.

Objectives: To distinguish between a dictionary, an encyclopedia, and an atlas in terms of the kind of information each contains. (Study Skills) To draw conclusions about the details of a selection. (Comprehension)

Remembering the Selection

Complete these sentences by underlining the correct ending.

1. "How to Build an Ant Village" is   **a.** fiction   **b.** <u>nonfiction</u>

2. Its main purpose is to   **a.** <u>instruct</u>   **b.** entertain

3. The information in the selection is   **a.** <u>factual</u>   **b.** make-believe

4. The information is presented in   **a.** <u>step-by-step order</u>   **b.** story plot

5. The word <u>colony</u> in this article means   **a.** <u>animals living together</u>   **b.** a new settlement

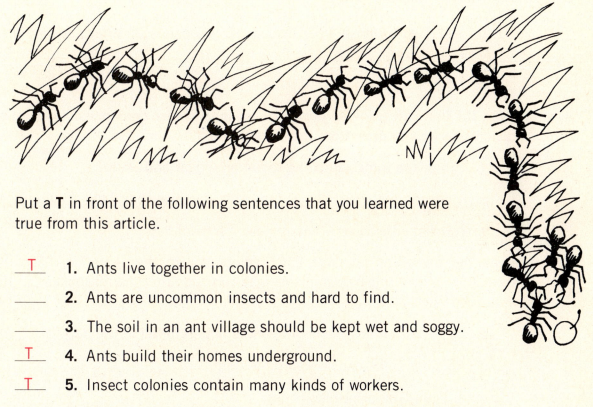

Put a **T** in front of the following sentences that you learned were true from this article.

 T 1. Ants live together in colonies.

_____ 2. Ants are uncommon insects and hard to find.

_____ 3. The soil in an ant village should be kept wet and soggy.

 T 4. Ants build their homes underground.

 T 5. Insect colonies contain many kinds of workers.

_____ 6. Ants are easily found in the muddy banks of rivers and lakes.

 T 7. Ants in an ant village will always have to be supplied with food and water.

_____ 8. Ants are the only kind of insects that live in colonies.

 T 9. Ants should be handled carefully.

_____ 10. Dark construction paper frightens ants.

_____ 11. Each worker in an ant colony does many different kinds of jobs.

Level 13: "How to Build an Ant Village" pp. 212-215.   **55**

Objective: To recall significant details from the selection. (Comprehension)

Drawing Conclusions

Put an "x" in the box next to the correct answer for each question below.

1. Read the first paragraph in "How to Build an Ant Village" on page 212. Of the following sentences, which would be a correct conclusion to draw from the information in the paragraph?

   ☐ a. Some workers in an ant colony are lazy.

   ☐ b. The easiest way to observe ants is to go outside where they live.

   ☒ c. It would be possible, but not as easy, to study colonies of bees, wasps, and termites.

2. Now read the paragraph which begins "You can discover many things about ants . . ." Which of these sentences would be a correct conclusion to draw from this paragraph?

   ☐ a. There's really no need to make an ant village since you can learn many things just by watching them around their ant hills.

   ☒ b. You need to make an ant village so you can learn what goes on in the ants' homes.

   ☐ c. No one should help you make your ant village.

3. Read the first paragraph on page 214. Which of these sentences states an accurate conclusion we can draw from this paragraph?

   ☒ a. Two of the things ants like to eat are sugar and water.

   ☐ b. It doesn't matter what you feed ants because they'll eat anything.

   ☐ c. You can only observe ants by using a hand lens.

4. Read the paragraph on page 214 beginning with the sentence, "The ants now have. . . ." From this paragraph we may conclude that the reason we put the paper around the jar is—

   ☒ a. Ants' natural home environment is underground in the dark.

   ☐ b. Ants don't like people watching them.

   ☐ c. Ants like the color black best.

5. Read the last paragraph in the selection on page 215. Which of the following statements would be a logical conclusion to draw from this paragraph?

   ☐ a. An ant colony in a jar will teach you all you need to know about ants.

   ☐ b. Facts about ants are interesting for children, but not important for adult scientists.

   ☒ c. Ants have a lot of information to give us and many people have studied and written about them.

Level 13: "How To Build an Ant Village" pp. 212-215.

Objective: To draw conclusions about the details of a selection. (Comprehension)

ORDERING DETAILS

What You'll Need

The list below gives some of the pieces of equipment needed to build an ant village. Match each piece with its use in the second column.

Equipment		Uses
window screen	e	**a.** to scoop up earth from anthill
mason jar	g	**b.** to study ants closely
funnel	h	**c.** food for the ants
hand lens	b	**d.** to cut window screen
moist sponge	f	**e.** to keep ants in jar
sugar, grass seed	c	**f.** moisture for the ants
black paper	i	**g.** contains the ant village
large spoon	a	**h.** to transfer ants from anthill to jar
scissors	d	**i.** to make the ant village dark

How You'll Do It

Number the sentences below in the order they should be followed when building an ant village.

5   Put the circles of screen on top of the jar.

8   Wrap black paper around the outside of the jar.

1   Get acquainted with ants by watching them outdoors.

3   Cut two circles of screen the size of the sealer lid.

7   Screw on the jar ring.

4   Find an ant hill and fill the jar ¾ full of earth.

6   Sprinkle water, grass seed, and sugar on top of earth.

2   Get a one-quart mason jar and remove the sealer lid.

Objectives: To demonstrate an understanding of the importance of order. (Study Skills) To recall details from the selection. (Comprehension)

FACTS AND FANCY

Read the following paragraphs. Then answer the questions.

A fly flew near Charlotte's web and landed on the barn wall. It folded back its two wings and listened to the conversation going on nearby.

"Well, I don't intend to get caught in that web like the other fellow," the fly muttered to itself. "All flies aren't that careless. We're among the fastest of all flying insects and can escape from a slow spider!"

The fly's eyes, made up of thousands of lenses, glistened in the dim barn light. The claws on the end of its legs dug into the wooden wall, holding the fly upside down.

"And besides," the fly thought greedily, "I can smell food coming from the pig's trough. I'll go sample that while he wastes his time discussing spiders and flies."

Like "Charlotte's Web," this little story is **fiction** but contains several **facts**. Read the following sentences. Put an **F** in front of each one that is **fact**.

_F_ **1.** Flies live in barns.

_____ **2.** They eavesdrop on conversations.

_F_ **3.** Flies have two wings.

_F_ **4.** They are among the fastest of all flying insects.

_____ **5.** Many flies are careless.

_F_ **6.** Fly's eyes are made up of thousands of lenses.

_F_ **7.** A fly has claws on the end of its legs.

_F_ **8.** Flies can walk upside down.

_____ **9.** Flies are greedy.

_____**10.** Flies don't waste time.

MATCHING CHARACTERISTICS AND CHARACTERS

Select words below that describe either Wilbur or Charlotte. Write them under the correct headings.

lonely	clever	unhappy	pretty	bold
shy	practical	witty	innocent	tender-hearted

Wilbur: _____ lonely, unhappy, shy, innocent, tender-hearted _____

Charlotte: _____ clever, pretty, bold, practical, witty _____

Level 13: "Charlotte's Web" pp. 216-223.

Objectives: To identify elements of fact within fiction writing. To describe a given character in a selection in terms of explicit and implicit character traits. (Comprehension)

SPEAKING IN IDIOMS

You know that an **idiom** is a word or phrase that means something different than the usual meaning of the words. Here are some sentences with idioms. Read each one. Then check the phrase below that gives the meaning of the idiom as it is used in that sentence.

1. We would have gone on a picnic yesterday, but it was <u>raining cats and dogs.</u>
   ____ animals fell from the sky
   ✓ it rained very hard

2. I may not be as <u>flashy</u> as some spiders, but I'll do.
   ____ turning on and off
   ✓ fancy, showy

3. It was an important meeting and she <u>broke her neck</u> to be on time.
   ____ had an accident on the way
   ✓ hurried

4. When I found out I was wrong, I had to <u>eat my words.</u>
   ✓ say I was sorry
   ____ chew some paper with words on it

5. A spider has to <u>pick up</u> a living somehow.
   ✓ to work for, to get
   ____ to grasp with one's hands

6. When I tried to pick up the robin's egg I was <u>all thumbs.</u>
   ✓ clumsy
   ____ had a hand with five thumbs

7. Catching insects in my web is not a bad <u>pitch</u>, really.
   ✓ way to do something
   ____ to throw a ball

8. When Rita won first prize, she was <u>walking on air.</u>
   ____ didn't touch the ground
   ✓ was very happy

9. If you're not careful, someone may <u>pull the wool over your eyes.</u>
   ✓ fool you
   ____ tie a wool scarf over your head

10. <u>Keep your eyes peeled</u> or we'll miss our stop on the bus.
    ____ peel off your eyelids
    ✓ keep alert

11. We'd better not let any <u>grass grow under our feet</u> if we want to make that train.
    ____ stand on newly planted grass seed
    ✓ make haste

12. I'm afraid everything I say to you is going <u>in one ear and out the other.</u>
    ✓ you're not paying attention
    ____ right through your head

USING AN ENCYCLO-PEDIA

Most of you have already used an encyclopedia many times. Listed below are a number of statements describing the content and arrangement of this important source of information. Choose words from the following list to complete each statement.

Index	volumes	spine	subjects
guide words	alphabetical	cross-reference	

1. While a dictionary provides information about a great number of words, an encyclopedia provides information about a great number of _____subjects_____ .

2. Both dictionaries and encyclopedias list their entries in _____alphabetical_____ order.

3. Because encyclopedia entries include much more information than dictionary entries, they usually have over twenty separate _____volumes_____ .

4. To help us locate information easily, each volume lists its number and the beginning letters of its first and last subject entry on the book's _____spine_____ .

5. Most encyclopedias also use _____guide words_____ at the top of each page to help us find specific subject headings.

6. Look at the illustration at the top of this page. In which of the pictured volumes would you expect to find specific information about the following animals?

___18___ **a.** spider   ___4___ **e.** crayfish

___7___ **b.** flamingo   ___21___ **f.** zebra

___19___ **c.** tarantula   ___13___ **g.** millipede

___1___ **d.** ant   ___15___ **h.** porpoise

Level 13: "Spider" pp. 224-225.

Objectives: To describe the form and function of an encyclopedia. To choose the correct encyclopedia volume for finding a particular topic. (Study Skills)

7. At the end of most encyclopedia entries or articles, readers are referred to other subject headings that they may use as a

<u>cross-reference</u>

8. Most encyclopedias also provide a special volume that lists the exact locations of all subject headings and their cross-references. This volume is called the

<u>Index</u>

9. At the end of an article on **porpoises** in *The World Book Encyclopedia* is the sentence:

See also **Dolphin; Killer whale; Whale.**

In what three volumes of the pictured encyclopedias would you expect to find additional information on the **porpoise?**

Letter
D
K
W

Volume number
5
11
21

10. Here is an entry from the combined Index volume of *The New Book of Knowledge* on the **trout.**

Trout, fish
  baits and lures **F** 206
  cutthroat trout, state fish of New Mexico **N** 185
  fish hatchery, Quebec, Canada, picture **C** 486
  locomotion **A** 290
  reproduction **R** 178, 179

		Vol.	Pages
a.	Where would you look to find a picture of a trout?	C	486
b.	Where would you look to find specific information on trout fishing?	F	206
c.	Where would you look to find out how a trout reproduces its species?	R	178, 179

Who-o-o?

Both animals and people play important parts in Vera Henry's "Ong, of Canada." Let's see how much you can remember about each of her seven story characters. First write the character's name under each picture. Then identify the character in "Ong, of Canada" that answers each of the following "Who" questions.

WHO-O-O-O?

1. walked with a crutch? ___the captain___

2. had a golden nose? ___Tavish___

3. had red hair? ___Mrs. Plumley___

4. had a red sports car? ___Johnny Salt___

5. tried to hatch a doorknob? ___Jessica___

6. loved to play with her pets? ___Holly___

7. baked excellent chocolate cakes? ___Mrs. Plumley___

8. had a long black neck and beautiful white feathers?
   ___Ong___

9. was called Little One? ___Holly___

10. was a good swimmer for his age? ___Tavish___

11. would have liked to have been an astronaut? ___the captain___

12. knew the ways of both poultices and antibiotics?
    ___Johnny Salt___

ONG

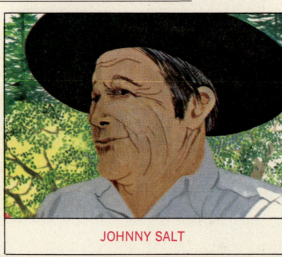

JOHNNY SALT

Level 13: "Ong, of Canada" pp. 228-245.

Objective: To describe characters in a selection in terms of explicit and implicit character traits. (Comprehension)

13. hissed and pecked at the front door, at tires, and at Mrs.

Plumley? _____ Ong _____

14. was loyal and brave? _____ Tavish _____

15. had a change of heart? _____ Mrs. Plumley _____

16. ate peanut butter and carrot sandwiches? _____ Holly _____

17. guided the boat skillfully?_____ Johnny Salt _____

18. wore bangs? _____ Holly _____

19. carved wooden figures?_____ the captain _____

20. was full of mischief? _____ Ong _____

On a separate sheet of paper, write a short description of one of your favorite characters in "Ong, of Canada." Do not use the name of the character in your paragraph. When you finish, see if your classmates can guess who your character is from the clues in your description. Include some description of what your character looks like and does. At the end tell why you especially liked this character.

JESSICA

MRS. PLUMLEY

THE CAPTAIN   HOLLY

TAVISH

Two Comic Characters

The feuding of Ong and Mrs. Plumley provides a number of humorous moments in "Ong, of Canada." Circle the letter of the word or words that best complete the sentences below.

1. Mrs. Plumley blamed Ong for a number of things. One of the first was for causing Holly to catch a _____ when she fell in the pond.

   a. frog   **b.** cold   **c.** rash

2. Ong, of course, did do some annoying things. Every day he used his beak to _____.

   a. knock at Mrs. Plumley's door   **b.** poke holes in Holly's lunch bag   **c.** make strange pecking noises

3. Mrs. Plumley annoyed Ong, too. He didn't like those odd _____ standing up around her head.

   a. ribbons   **b.** combs   **c.** red feathers

4. Mrs. Plumley also had a habit of waving either her apron or her _____ at Ong.

   a. frying pan   **b.** broom   **c.** dish towel

5. Sometimes Ong would tease Mrs. Plumley by taking small bites out of her _____.

   a. green tomatoes   **b.** freshly baked bread   **c.** favorite slippers

6. One warm June day Mrs. Plumley was chasing Ong, but this time Ong _____.

   a. didn't pay any attention   **b.** got really scared   **c.** had had enough

7. Instead of running from Mrs. Plumley, Ong turned, started running toward her, and _____.   **a.** snuck into the house ahead of her   **b.** took a small nip from her plump leg   **c.** pushed her right into the pond

Level 13: "Ong, of Canada" pp. 228-245.
Objective: To identify humorous elements in a selection. (Comprehension)

WHAT IS IT LIKE?

Authors frequently use similes to help readers picture the characters and actions in their stories. A simile describes one thing as being like another. For example, not all of us may have heard wild geese, but when their "racket" is described as being "like a jammed automobile horn," we get a pretty good idea why the noise irritated Mrs. Plumley.

Vera Henry has used a number of lively and humorous similes in "Ong, of Canada." Turn back to the pages listed below and see if you can complete each of the following comparisons. After you have written the author's simile, see if you can write a lively one of your own. The first one is done for you.

	On page	this . . .	was compared to	this . . .
1.	229	the racket of the wild geese	AUTHOR'S SIMILE	a jammed automobile horn
			YOUR OWN	kids at recess
2.	229	Mrs. Plumley crying, "Shoo! Shoo!"	AUTHOR'S SIMILE	a loud mosquito
			YOUR OWN	Answers will vary.
3.	230	Ong's hissing at Mrs. Plumley	AUTHOR'S SIMILE	a leaky tire
			YOUR OWN	
4.	231	Ong's neck	AUTHOR'S SIMILE	the hose on a vacuum cleaner
			YOUR OWN	
5.	240	the bulldozers and workers on shore	AUTHOR'S SIMILE	toys
			YOUR OWN	

Level 13: "Ong, of Canada" pp. 228-245.

Objective: To explore examples of similes in a selection. (Comprehension)

65

People and Careers

Look over the articles on pages 226-227 and pages 248-249. Then complete the sentences with one of these words.

insects   eggs   helpful   bacteria

hives   veils   shelter   vaccine

1. Beekeepers set up _____hives_____ for bees to use as homes.

2. Beekeepers protect themselves from being stung by wearing _____veils_____ and other special clothing.

3. Entomologists are scientists who study _____insects_____.

4. Some insects are harmful to plants and animals and some are _____helpful_____.

5. Poultry farmers must give their flocks food and _____shelter_____.

6. One way of earning a living as a poultry farmer is by selling _____eggs_____.

7. A _____vaccine_____ can help prevent certain diseases.

8. Very tiny germs that can cause certain diseases are called _____bacteria_____.

Match the names of the following people with the sentences below. Write the correct letter in front of each sentence.

a. Ernest E. Just   **c.** John James Audubon
b. John Muir   **d.** Jessie I. Price

___d___ 1. This person is a bacteriologist who developed an important animal vaccine.

___b___ 2. This person helped make Sequoia National Park possible.

___d___ 3. This scientist's work was important to the duck-farming industry.

___a___ 4. This scientist was one of the first people to study how one-celled eggs develop.

___c___ 5. This person painted over four hundred life-size pictures of North American birds.

___b___ 6. This person has a national redwood forest named in his honor.

___c___ 7. This person has a famous wildlife society named in his honor.

Level 13: "From Cells to Sequoias," "Close-Up on Insects" pp. 226-227; "Bird Artist," "Chicks and Ducks" pp. 248-249.
Objective: To recall significant details from selections. To demonstrate understanding of special vocabulary from selections. (Comprehension)

WORDS, WORDS, WORDS

Match the words on the left with the short definitions on the right.
Write the correct letter in front of each word.

d	1. mystery	**a.**	wild area with no people living in it
j	2. laboratory	**b.**	giant evergreen tree
f	3. poultry	**c.**	arrangement; organization
h	4. cells	**d.**	unknown; a puzzle
b	5. sequoia	**e.**	protect; a protected place
i	6. investigate	**f.**	chickens, ducks, geese, turkeys, etc.
a	7. wilderness	**g.**	a person's work, job, profession
c	8. structure	**h.**	smallest units of living matter
e	9. preserve	**i.**	look into, study
g	10. career	**j.**	scientific workshop

Complete the following sentences with one of the words above.

1. John Muir helped to _____preserve_____ our country's giant redwood and _____sequoia_____ trees from destruction.

2. A farmer who raises chickens and ducks is called a _____poultry_____ farmer.

3. Living things are made up of millions of _____cells_____.

4. Scientists often carry out experiments in a _____laboratory_____.

5. The scientist is trying to find out about a _____mystery_____ in nature.

6. Our government has set aside millions of acres of _____wilderness_____ where plants and animals live naturally.

7. Scientists like Ernest Just _____investigate_____ the mysteries of nature to try and solve them.

8. Ernest Just studied the different parts of a cell or a cell's _____structure_____.

9. Two _____career_____s that deal with animals are beekeeper and poultry farmer.

Level 13: "From Cells to Sequoias," "Close-Up on Insects," pp. 226-227; "Bird Artist," "Chicks and Ducks" pp. 248-249.

67

Objective: To demonstrate understanding of special vocabulary from selections. (Comprehension)

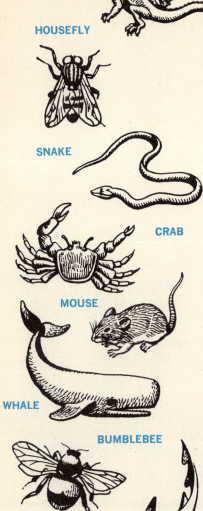

LIZARD

HOUSEFLY

SNAKE

CRAB

MOUSE

WHALE

BUMBLEBEE

SHARK

TUNA

MOSQUITO

EAGLE

LION

MAKING GROUPS

You know that things can be **classified** into **categories**. This is done by grouping items according to what they have in common. There is an almost endless number of ways to classify things. Look at the pictures of animals on these two pages. Then group them according to the directions below.

Have You Seen It?

In the left-hand column write the names of animals you have seen. In the right-hand column, write the names of animals you may have seen in pictures, but have not seen yourself.

Animals You Have Seen	Animals You Have Not Seen
Answers will vary	

What's Its Name?

Group the names of these animals into categories depending on the number of syllables in each word.

One syllable: snake, crab, mouse, whale, shark, sheep, shrimp, bass

Two syllables: housefly, lizard, tuna, eagle, lion, swallow, goldfish, lobster, parrot, turtle

Three syllables: bumblebee, mosquito, barnacle, butterfly

Four syllables: alligator

Five syllables: Canadian goose

Level 13: "The Animal Parade" pp. 250-254.

Objective: To sort and classify items according to a specific common feature. (Study Skills)

What Does It Look Like?

Group the animals by the number of legs they have. Two group headings have been given. Decide what the other two headings should be. Use an encyclopedia if you need help.

No legs	Two legs
snake	eagle
whale	swallow
shark	Canadian goose
tuna	parrot
goldfish	
barnacle	
bass	

Four legs	More than four legs
lizard	housefly
mouse	crab
lion	bumblebee
sheep	mosquito
alligator	lobster
turtle	butterfly
	shrimp

Imagining

Pretend you are writing stories about these animals and need to decide what they are like. On a separate sheet of paper, group the animals into the two following categories:

Timid, Gentle Animals   Bold, Daring Animals

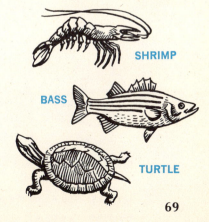

69

See How Fast They Run!

Here is a graph showing the average top speed of some familiar animals. Study the graph and then answer the questions on the next page.

CHEETAH

	48 kph (30 mph)	64 kph (40 mph)	72 kph (45 mph)	80 kph (50 mph)	110 kph (70 mph)

SNAKE
3 kph (2 mph)

CAT   GREYHOUND   OSTRICH   RACEHORSE   JACKRABBIT   DEER

Level 13: "The Animal Parade" pp. 250-254.

Objective: To read and understand graphs. (Study Skills)

1. As you read from left to right on the graph, does the speed of the animals increase or decrease? _____ increase _____

2. Which animal on the graph moves the fastest at its top speed? _____ cheetah _____

3. Which animal moves the slowest? _____ snake _____

4. Which animal on the graph runs 48 kilometers an hour? _____ cat _____

5. How fast does a jackrabbit run? _____ 72 kilometers per hour _____

6. Do the sizes of the animals affect their speeds? _____ No, _____
   some large animals, such as the elephant, don't run as fast as smaller ones.

7. The African elephant runs 40 kilometers per hour. Between what two animals on the graph should it be placed? _____ between the snake and the cat _____

8. Here are the average adult weights of more familiar animals. Using the space below, make a graph arranging these animals by weight. Start with the smallest at the left of the graph and the largest at the right.

camel	500 kilograms (1,100 pounds)
pig	91 kilograms (200 pounds)
sheep	68 kilograms (150 pounds)
chimpanzee	82 kilograms (180 pounds)
giraffe	910 kilograms (2,000 pounds)
chicken	2.6 kilograms (6.5 pounds)

Every day we meet many new words. Most of the time we are able to guess the meaning of these words without going to the dictionary. How are we able to do this? We use the other words in the sentence — that is, the **sentence context** — to give us clues to the new word's meaning.

Here are eight sentences taken from Donald Culross Peattie's "The Animal Parade." In each sentence one word has been underlined. Read the sentence; then decide which of the three words at the right would make the most sense if it were substituted for the underlined word. Underline your answer. Use a dictionary if you need help.

MORE CLUES TO MEANING

Original Sentence	**Words for Substitution**
1. How long they live <u>varies</u>.	<u>differs</u> increases depends
2. Length is no <u>measure</u> for life.	distance <u>standard</u> length
3. The field mouse itself finds life too much for it before it can <u>finish</u> its second winter.	suspect <u>end</u> begin
4. But <u>soaring</u> over mountains and forests, it reaches heights of adventure and experience impossible to the salamanders.	creeping climbing <u>flying</u>
5. The winners of the great game of <u>endurance</u> are admired.	victory contest <u>survival</u>
6. It is better, people will feel, to stand <u>upright</u> on two feet.	firmly <u>erect</u> correctly
7. Every year discoveries in medicine and science <u>prolong</u> human life.	endanger shorten <u>extend</u>
8. We may well give thanks for our own <u>share</u> of the grand adventure.	<u>part</u> division slice

Level 13: "The Animal Parade" pp. 250-254.

Objective: To use context clues to determine the meaning of special vocabulary in a selection. (Comprehension)

THE UNIT IN REVIEW

After each of the following titles from this unit, write either
F for **fiction** or N for **nonfiction**. Then answer the questions.

1. "Ong, of Canada"   F   5. "The Animal Parade"   N

2. "Spider"   N   6. "Bird Artist"   N

3. "Chicks and Ducks"   N   7. "Charlotte's Web"   F

4. "Haiku"   F   8. "Señor Billy Goat"   F

9. Which of these selections is an encyclopedia article? _____ "Spider" _____

10. Which is a Puerto Rican folktale? _____ "Señor Billy Goat" _____

11. Which is a biographical sketch? _____ "Bird Artist" _____

12. Which is an essay with facts and opinions? _____ "The Animal Parade" _____

Decide if the following books and titles are likely to be **fiction** or **nonfiction**.
Write F for fiction and N for nonfiction.

1. A mathematics book N   8. An atlas of Spanish maps N

2. Grimm's Fairy Tales F   9. A United States history book N

3. "Life in the Year 2088" F   10. An encyclopedia N

4. "Clothing Worn in 1880" N   11. "How to Repair a Wagon" N

5. A book about computers N   12. A Swedish cookbook N

6. "The Invisible Robot" F   13. Faraway Folk Tales F

7. "Photographs of Maine" N   14. A French/English dictionary N

Write the title of a fiction book you have read recently: _____ Answers will vary. _____

_____

Write the title of a nonfiction book you have read recently: _____

_____

Objective: To distinguish between fiction and nonfiction writing. (Comprehension)

MAIN IDEA AND DETAILS

The sentences below tell about six selections from Unit 3. Write the letter of the title in front of the sentence that gives the correct main idea.

a. "Ong, of Canada" **b.** "Señor Billy Goat" **c.** "James Henry Trotter and

d. "Charlotte's Web" **e.** "How to Build an   the Fantastic Peach"

f. "Spider"   Ant Village"

b   An old couple gets help from a tiny visitor.

d   A pig finds a surprising new friend.

c   A boy has a fabulous adventure with five amazing new friends.

a   A girl raises a wild animal as a pet.

f   Facts about a small animal.

e   A how-to article on performing an experiment with insects.

Complete the following statements by thinking back to the selections you've read. Choose from among these words for your answers.

web	enemies	ant	animals
peasants	bolas	mixture	colonies

1. James Henry Trotter's adventure began when an old man gave him a strange _____mixture_____ in a paper bag.

2. The farmers María and Ramón were _____peasants_____.

3. Their problem was solved by la Hormiguita, an _____ant_____.

4. Ants are insects that live in _____colonies_____.

5. When Wilbur met Charlotte, she was in her _____web_____.

6. In "Ong, of Canada," Ong and Mrs. Plumley started out as _____enemies_____.

7. One kind of spider that does not spin a web is the _____bolas_____ spider.

8. Living things that are not plants are usually called _____animals_____.

Objectives: To recall the main ideas of selections. To recall significant details from selections. (Comprehension)

FACT OR OPINION

Write F after the following statements if they are **facts** and O if they are **opinions**.

1. The sequoia is an evergreen.   F
2. Sequoia National Park is in California.   F
3. Sequoias are the loveliest of trees.   O
4. Sequoia is said si kwoi´ə.   F
5. Most spiders spin webs.   F
6. Spiders are interesting.   O
7. Spiders have eight legs.   F
8. There is a spider web in the corner of our garage.   F
9. Spider webs in garages should be removed.   O
10. John Audubon drew birds.   F
11. He was an excellent artist.   O
12. The American Audubon Society is named after Audubon.   F
13. It's a worthy organization.   O
14. Sparrows live in our trees.   F
15. I saw five sparrows in the bird bath this morning.   F
16. Sparrows chirp sweetly.   O
17. Birds are nicer to look at than spiders.   O
18. Poultry farming is fun.   O
19. The forecast for tomorrow is snow.   F
20. It looks as if it will rain.   O
21. It rained three days this week already.   F

Two Viewpoints

In this unit we've looked at "the wonder of life" from both the scientific and the imaginative points of view. Now choose one of your favorite animals and write two paragraphs about it. In the first paragraph, write as if you were a scientist recording only factual information about the animal's physical appearance, natural home, eating habits, etc. In the second, write about your animal as it might be described playing the hero or heroine in an adventure tale. This time when you tell how your animal looks, eats, and lives, let your imagination go free.

Objective: To distinguish between fact and opinion. (Comprehension) To demonstrate an understanding of contrasting points of view through creative writing. (Comprehension)

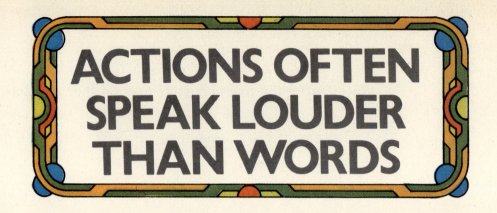

ACTIONS OFTEN SPEAK LOUDER THAN WORDS

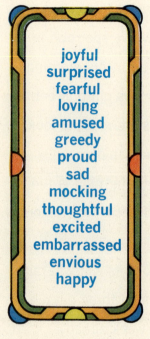

joyful
surprised
fearful
loving
amused
greedy
proud
sad
mocking
thoughtful
excited
embarrassed
envious
happy

Our actions often say a great deal about our thoughts and feelings. In "The Magic Bagpipe" Gerry and George Armstrong seldom tell us what their characters are thinking or feeling; instead, they let the character's behavior speak for itself. We aren't told, for example, that when MacSkirl first saw Donald's beautiful new pipes, he was full of envy and greed. But the description of his actions, beginning with "The old man stared from beneath his bushy eyebrows," leaves us with little doubt of his feelings.

Below and on page 77 are seven passages from the story. Each passage tells about one or more of the characters' actions. After reading the sentences, choose words from the illustration at the left that you think describe the thoughts and feelings of the character at this time in the story. A number of words are possible in most cases. But choose only the words that would go with the actions that are given.

Character's Actions	Character's Thoughts and Feelings
1. "And what did MacSkirl do but jerk Donald's pipes from him and shove his own bagpipes at the boy!"	envious, greedy, excited
2. "At first the crowd listened in silence. Then someone tittered and someone else giggled. And in a moment the whole crowd was rocking with laughter."	surprised, amused, mocking
3. "The pipes fell from his [MacSkirl's] shaking hands. He pulled his bonnet down over his ears and fled."	embarrassed, fearful

Level 13: "The Magic Bagpipe" pp. 262-267.

Objective: To describe a given character in terms of explicit and implicit character traits. (Comprehension)

4. "The crowd grew very quiet as Donald paced slowly up and down, and the music sang of hardship and loneliness and disappointment."

thoughtful,

sad

5. "Then Donald quickened his step, and the people lifted their heads as his music changed.... People began to tap their feet and nod and smile."

proud,

happy

6. "People cheered and screamed and stamped their feet. Bonnets flew into the air."

joyful,

excited,

proud

7. "And then Donald's parents were beside him. His father clapped him...on the shoulder, his mother hugged him, and his little sister jumped up and down...."

proud, loving,

excited, happy

SYNONYMS AND SPECIAL SOUNDS

MEANING IN CONTEXT

Locate each story word below on its listed page. Then decide which word in the second column comes closest to the meaning of the word as it is used in the story. Underline the word.

Page	Story Words	Possible Synonyms		
262	celebration	<u>party</u>	meeting	parade
262	realized	appeared	<u>knew</u>	remembered
262	struggling	<u>trying</u>	running	quarreling
262	competitions	classes	<u>contests</u>	conversation
263	munched	squashed	<u>ate</u>	cracked
264	jerk	<u>grab</u>	take	lift
264	shove	kick	<u>push</u>	throw
265	bewildered	amused	proud	<u>confused</u>
266	paced	skipped	<u>stepped</u>	stood
266	overcome	forgot	accept	<u>conquer</u>

WORDS THAT MAKE NOISE

One of the words following each question below does not belong in the answer. Draw a line through the incorrect word.

1. Which of the following things would not **squeal?**   pigs   tires   ~~drums~~

2. Which would not **gurgle?**   water bottle   ~~book~~   stomach

3. Which person would probably not **wheeze?**

   ~~person with measles~~   person with chest cold   person with whooping cough

4. Which would not **shriek?**   birds   ~~tigers~~   children

5. Which wouldn't make a person **gasp?**

   a sudden shock   lack of air   ~~a boring story~~

6. Which wouldn't make a person **hoarse?**

   ~~too much dancing~~   too much singing   too much talking

7. Which of the following would not **roar?**   fire   ~~piano~~   crowd

Level 13: "The Magic Bagpipe" pp. 262-267.

Objectives: To use context clues to determine the meaning of a word. To identify semantic relationships. (Comprehension)

DETECTING DEFINITIONS

Here are ten words from "Bola and the Oba's Drummers" that may be new or unfamiliar to you. Two short definitions follow each word. Only one is correct. Before using the dictionary, find the word on its listed page and try to decide from its use in the story context which definition applies. Put an **X** before the correct definition. Remember that it is sometimes helpful to read several sentences surrounding a given word before trying to guess its meaning.

Page	Word	Meaning in Context
1. 273	**scornfully**	_X_ **a.** with a sneer
		___ **b.** with a smile
2. 274	**sought**	_X_ **a.** looked for
		___ **b.** discovered
3. 274	**bell-studded**	___ **a.** bell-constructed
		_X_ **b.** bell-covered
4. 275	**feeble**	___ **a.** energetic
		_X_ **b.** weak
5. 276	**gingerly**	_X_ **a.** carefully
		___ **b.** carelessly
6. 276	**thongs**	___ **a.** chips
		_X_ **b.** strips
7. 277	**chambers**	_X_ **a.** special rooms
		___ **b.** special roads
8. 277	**beckoning**	_X_ **a.** motioning to come
		___ **b.** waving good-bye
9. 278	**veranda**	___ **a.** forest
		_X_ **b.** porch
10. 281	**gleaming**	___ **a.** wet
		_X_ **b.** glowing

Level 13: "Bola and the Oba's Drummers" pp. 272-288.

Objective: To use context clues to determine the meaning of a word. (Comprehension)

20 Questions

Underline the word or words in blue that accurately complete the statements under each heading.

Reading Classification

1. "Bola and the Oba's Drummers" may be classified as a piece of fiction—nonfiction.

2. This means that the events in the story are—are not true.

3. Because "Bola and the Oba's Drummers" is part of a larger book, it is called an excerpt—extension.

4. The events in "Bola and the Oba's Drummers" are more realistic—fantastic than the events in "The Magic Bagpipe."

5. This means that the events probably could—could not happen in real life.

Story Setting

6. "Bola and the Oba's Drummers" takes place in Africa—Asia — Australia.

7. The story events all occur in a country called Niagara—Nigeria—Nairobi

8. Most of the story takes place in Ado-Ido village—the marketplace—the palace courtyard.

9. The story probably is dated in the present or the recent past because the boys are familiar with the sport of baseball—football—basketball.

10. The action in the story takes place on two different market days spanning one week—two weeks—one month in time.

Story Characters

11. The two **major characters** in "Bola and the Oba's Drummers" are Bola and the Oba—Tunji—Bamiji.

12. Every other market day Father Ayan—Chief Adepoju—the Oba has a council meeting in his palace.

Objective: To identify and describe literary elements of form, setting, characterization, and plot. (Comprehension/Literary Skills)

13. The Oba—Father Ayan—Bamiji has a superior look and speaks scornfully when he tells Bola, "One must be born a drummer."

14. Tunji—Chief Adepoju—Kanango has a merry, narrow face and speaks kindly when he tells Bola, "If you want, I will teach you to drum."

15. At the end of the story Bola is able to make Iya Ilu—Ishaju—Kanango say his name.

The Plot and Theme

16. The **plot** of a story might be compared to a **plan** of the story's main description—symbols—events.

17. The **theme** might be compared to a **message** about the story's main idea—facts—setting.

18. Many story plots begin with a basic **problem** that the main character wishes to solve. In "Bola and the Oba's Drummers," Bola's problem is
    a. he wants to learn to play the drums and make them talk.
    b. he wants to be sure he will return to the market-place.
    c. he wants to become the Oba.

19. In most plots a series of events leads to a **climax** or **turning point** in the story where we no longer wonder if the main character will solve his problem. In "Bola and the Oba's Drummers," the climax comes when
    a. Bola returns a second time to the palace.
    b. Bola is able to make his drum say his name.
    c. Bola enters the drum room in the palace walls.

20. The main **theme** or **lesson about life** in "Bola and the Oba's Drummers" might be stated:
    a. Life is more exciting in the "great towns" than in the "small villages."
    b. You cannot learn certain skills, you must be born with them.
    c. A new skill is learned most easily when there is determination, encouragement, patience, and practice.

INFORMATION, PLEASE...

Encyclopedias and dictionaries are both valuable resource books. Read each sentence below. If the sentence tells something about an encyclopedia, write an E on the line in front of the sentence. If it tells something about a dictionary, write a D on the line. If the description fits both, write D and E on the line.

__E__ 1. It has many volumes.

__D__ 2. It has one volume.

__D,E__ 3. It is arranged in alphabetical order.

__D__ 4. It has a short entry containing the correct spelling, pronunciation, and one or more definitions of a word.

__E__ 5. It has a longer entry (one or more paragraphs) often with subheadings, several illustrations, and a list of related topics and other sources to read.

__E__ 6. It has extensive photographs (many in color), diagrams, maps, graphs, and charts.

__D__ 7. It has only occasional drawings and diagrams (usually in black and white).

__D__ 8. It contains a guide and a pronunciation key.

__E__ 9. It contains a separate guide and index.

__D,E__ 10. It is not intended to be read from beginning to end.

__D__ 11. It is used to find brief information about a given word.

__E__ 12. It is used to find detailed information about a certain topic—usually a special person, event, place, or thing.

Place a D or E or both on the line in front of the following items to indicate where you would go to find the needed information.

__E__ Names of African tribes   __E__ Different kinds of drums

__D__ The pronunciation of *veranda*   __D,E__ Who speaks the Yoruba language?

__E__ Nigerian animal wildlife   __D__ The spelling of the word /sə pir′ ē ər/

Objective: To describe the basic format of an encyclopedia. To compare an encyclopedia to a dictionary.

LIKE and AS

A. *Like* and *as* are two words used in comparisons called similes. Look at the pictures of the "Animals in Art" on the pages listed below. Then add words to complete the similes that follow. Try to think of more than one comparison for each simile.

Page		Simile

289   **1.** The lions' eyes look like _spotlights, searchlights,_ _headlights, beacons, stars_ shining in the night.

290   **2.** The animals on the cave wall appear like _visions in a dream,_ _pictures in a storybook, worn-out stuffed animals_ .

291   **3.** Compared to the size of the little horse, the ceremonial drum looks as big as a _house, whale, rocket ship, blimp_ .

292-293   **4.** The action of the dance might be described as having heat and energy like _a volcano, boiling liquid, crackling flames, thunder and lightning,_ _exploding fireworks_ .

295   **5.** The lunging elephants look as powerful and fast as _trucks, tanks, locomotives, trains, rocket ships_ .

296   **6.** The boy is removing the fleas as carefully as a _jeweler, seamstress,_ _tailor, sculptor, weaver, painter, wood carver_ working at a master craft.

296-297   **7.** The horses struggle like _fish on a hook, teams playing tug-of-war,_ _wrestlers in a ring_ .

B. Choose another picture from "Animals in Art" or look around your classroom for a picture or scene you find interesting. Then write a sentence in which you compare one thing in the picture to another thing that it reminds you of. _Answers will vary._

_____

_____

Level 13: "Animals in Art" pp. 289-300.
Objective: To construct similes.

83

A CHART FOR ART

The chart below helps us organize and compare information on seven pictures and paragraph captions presented in "Animals in Art." Review the seven pictures and their paragraphs on pages 289–300. Then complete the chart by choosing words from the following categories and writing them in the appropriate boxes. Some of the words, such as <u>unknown</u>, may be used more than once.

Note: The abbreviation **C.** under **TIME** stands for **century**. **B.C.** stands for **before Christ**.

ARTIST	PLACE	TIME	ART FORM	MATERIALS
Bonheur	Spain	6th C. B.C.	painting	wood
Ter Borch	Italy	16th C.	sculpture	oil colors
Picasso	India	17th C.		bronze
unknown	N. W. Africa	19th C.		
Rousseau	Holland	20th C.		
	France			

BACKGROUND INFORMATION ON SEVEN WORKS OF ART

WORK OF ART	ARTIST	PLACE	TIME	ART FORM	MATERIAL
Baboon and Young	Picasso	Spain	20th C.	sculpture	bronze
Boy Taking Fleas Out of a Dog	Ter Borch	Holland	17th C.	painting	oil colors
Drum from the Baga Tribe	unknown	N. W. Africa	20th C.	sculpture	wood
The Dream	Rousseau	France	19th C.	painting	oil colors
The Horse Fair	Bonheur	France	19th C.	painting	oil colors
Plowman of Arezzo	unknown	Italy	6th C. B.C.	sculpture	bronze
Akbar in Battle	unknown	India	16th C.	painting	oil colors

Level 13: "Animals in Art" pp. 289-300.

Objective: To organize and compare information. (Study Skills)

"TIME FOR FUN"

Read the poem below that describes many of the things that fun is in the picture essay "Time for Fun." Then find each picture named in the list below in your book. Decide which of the pictures is an example of the kind of fun that is named in the poem. Write the numbers of the pictures on the appropriate lines at the right of each stanza. There may be more than one example for each line in the poem.

1. Dream Ride
2. Children's Games
3. Footrace
4. Football Players

5. The Soap Bubble Blowers
6. Child's Game
7. Old Stagecoach
8. One Hundred Children at Play

Fun is . . .	Picture number
Country days in summertime,	6
Horses tugging at the reins,	1, 7
Bubble blowers blowing bubbles,	5
And a thousand different games!	2, 8
Sticks and bricks and stones and barrels,	2
One hundred children at play,	8
Dancing, prancing, rolling hoops,	6, 7, 8
Racing through the day.	2, 3, 4
Dressing up, acting out,	
Let's pretend and make-believe,	2, 7, 8
A magic coach, a rocking horse	1, 7
And a thousand different dreams.	1, 7

Level 13: "Time for Fun" pp. 301-312.

Objective: To locate information in a book. (Study Skills)

All libraries try to arrange books so they can be easily found by readers. To do this, libraries divide books into two main groups: **fiction** and **nonfiction.** Each group is in a different section of the library.

The fiction books are arranged on the shelves alphabetically by the author's last name. In most libraries, a fiction book has the letter **F** at the bottom of the spine.

The nonfiction books are arranged by subjects, such as art, astronomy, or history. They are also given special numbers to help organize them.

Here are some books of **fiction.** Number them in the order in which they would appear on the library shelves.

__3__ Ruth Chew, *What the Witch Left*

__5__ Nicholas Gray, *The Apple Stone*

__6__ Andre Norton, *Dragon Magic*

__10__ E.B. White, *Trumpet of the Swan*

__2__ Clyde Bulla, *Sword in the Tree*

__1__ Pearl Buck, *The Big Wave*

__9__ Barbara Wallace, *Claudia*

__4__ Roald Dahl, *Fantastic Mr. Fox*

__8__ Eve Titus, *The Two Stonecutters*

__7__ Anna Sewell, *Black Beauty*

Card catalogs are used in libraries to help readers find books. Card catalogs are drawers of cards. Each book in the library is usually listed on three different cards: a title card, an author card, and a subject card.

Author card:
Gives the author's name first and is arranged alphabetically by this name.

Title card:
Gives the book title first and is arranged alphabetically by this title.

Subject Card:
Gives the subject of the book first and is arranged alphabetically by this subject.

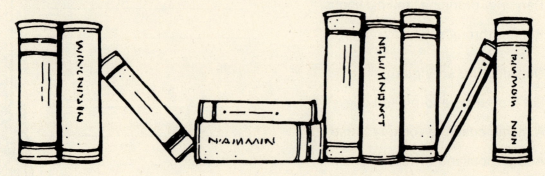

Objective: To demonstrate and describe the use of the library card catalog to obtain information in terms of title, author, and subject cards, and alphabetical arrangement of cards. (Study Skills)

Henry, Vera *Ong, the Wild Gander* J. B. Lippincott Co., 1966	**Author Card**

781 H

Hughes, Langston
The First Book of Jazz
Franklin Watts, Inc., 1954

Ong, the Wild Gander Henry, Vera J. B. Lippincott Co., 1966	**Title Card**

781 H

First Book of Jazz, The
Hughes, Langston
Franklin Watts, Inc., 1954

Animal Stories Henry, Vera *Ong, the Wild Gander* J. B. Lippincott Co., 1966	**Subject Card**

781 H

Jazz Music
Hughes, Langston
The First Book of Jazz
Franklin Watts, Inc., 1954

Answer these questions about the card catalog.

1. Who wrote *Ong, the Wild Gander?*
   Vera Henry

2. Is it fiction or nonfiction?
   fiction

3. Where would you look to see if Vera Henry wrote other books?
   under H for Henry

4. How could you find other books about birds in the library?
   look under B for Birds

5. Who wrote *The First Book of Jazz?*
   Langston Hughes

6. Where would you look to find other books on jazz?
   under J for Jazz or under M for Music

7. Where would you look to find books on other kinds of music? under M for Music or under the letters that begin each kind of music, such as F for Folk Music

8. Where in the card catalog would you look to find books on musical instruments? under I for Instruments or M for Musical Instruments

9. Under what letter would you find books by Pearl Buck? B

10. In what three places could you look for *All About Bicycles* by T. Harpin?
    under H for T. Harpin;
    A for All About Bicycles;
    B for a subject card on bicycles

Reading a Play

Reading a play is quite different from reading a story. Open your book to the play on pages 313-329. Examine each page of the play. Then complete the following statements by underlining the words or phrases written in blue.

1. Unlike a story, a play begins with a list of characters—description of the setting— summary of the plot.

2. The **place and time** in which the play is supposed to be happening is the cast— character—setting.

3. Reference to the **curtain falling** on the last page of the play means that the play is a comedy—a tragedy—over.

4. The name of the setting is followed by a **paragraph description** of the scenery—the costumes—the opening action.

5. Once the play begins, it is written completely in dialogue—narration—description.

6. Each character's **lines** are signaled by quotation marks—the character's name— parentheses.

7. **Stage directions** are written in italics within quotation marks—parentheses—the character's name.

8. A common stage direction is written **(Ad lib).** It means make up a line as you go along—exit from the stage—add emphasis.

Read the sentences below. Put a P on the line in front of each sentence that tells something about a play.

___P___ It begins with a list of characters.

___P___ Stage directions describe the action.

_____ Each character's lines are written in quotation marks followed by *he said* or *she said*.

___P___ A character's lines follow that character's name.

_____ A play is divided into parts called chapters.

Level 13: "Atlanta" pp. 313-329.
Objective: To describe and identify the elements of the play form. (Literary Skills)

Acting in a Play

An actor makes the words of a play come alive by showing a character's actions and feelings. Read the lines below as though they are from a play. Then choose words from the bottom of the page that describe the kind of expression and gesture you think an actor should use to say each line. Write the word or words in the blanks at the right following each group of lines.

Lines	Kind of Expression and Gestures
1. This game is fun! Let's play it again.	excited, happy
2. You dropped that vase. You broke it!	angry, sad, tearful
3. Run for your lives! Run! Run!	excited, frightened
4. Don't be frightened. It's all right.	reassuring, confident
5. I don't know if that is such a good idea.	doubtful, worried
6. I will climb that mountain. I will try until I succeed!	serious, determined
7. Are you sure that it's safe up here?	worried, doubtful
8. Hurray! We did it! Hurray!	excited, proud, happy
9. Oh, no! I've lost my money!	tearful, sad
10. Calm down everyone. We'll be safe here.	reassuring, confident
11. Well done. You did a great job.	proud, happy
12. I heard a noise. What could it be?	frightened, suspicious
13. Welcome home!	excited, happy
14. Are you sure that you are okay?	worried, doubtful

tearful   sad   worried   serious   suspicious   determined   angry   frightened
alert   confident   reassuring   proud   happy   surprised   excited   doubtful

Level 13: "Atalanta" pp. 313-329.
Objective: To recognize nuances of meaning due to choice of words. (Comprehension)

SYNONYMS AND ANTONYMS

In English we have many words that have similar meanings or what we sometimes call **synonyms**. Here are two columns of words from **Time To Wonder**. When the words in the columns are correctly matched, you will have fifteen synonym pairs. Write the number of each word in the first column on the line before the word that shares the same or nearly the same meaning in the second column.

In English we also have many words that are just the opposite in meaning, or what we often call **antonyms**. Now match the ten antonym pairs in the following two columns. Write the number of each word in the first column before the letter of its antonym in the second column. If any of the words seem unfamiliar, use a dictionary.

1. clue	_2_ fast	**1.** timid	_12_ dark
2. swift	_9_ correct	**2.** raise	_5_ slow
3. ancestors	_6_ lift	**3.** enormous	_2_ lower
4. timid	_5_ bright	**4.** fragile	_11_ dull
5. clever	_7_ huge	**5.** swift	_7_ shorten
6. raise	_8_ breakable	**6.** empty	_14_ shout
7. enormous	_1_ hint	**7.** prolong	_9_ save
8. fragile	_10_ snug	**8.** morning	_3_ tiny
9. accurate	_3_ forefathers	**9.** destroy	_15_ very happy
10. cozy	_4_ shy	**10.** winner	_10_ loser
11. miserable	_12_ envious	**11.** exciting	_6_ full
12. jealous	_15_ scare	**12.** light	_13_ unknown
13. prolong	_11_ very unhappy	**13.** famous	_8_ evening
14. rare	_13_ stretch out	**14.** murmur	_4_ sturdy
15. terrify	_14_ unusual	**15.** miserable	_1_ bold

Level 13: "Atalanta" pp. 313-329.

Objective: To identify and describe synonyms and antonyms. (Language Skills)

Adjective or Adverb?

Complete the following sentences by writing the letter of the words below.

a. rather   **c.** verbs   **e.** quite   **g.** -ly

b. add   **d.** very   **f.** nouns   **h.** detail

Adjectives are words that describe __f__. Adverbs are words that tell more about __c__. Many adverbs are made by adding the ending __g__ to adjectives. Adjectives and adverbs both __b__ meaning to a sentence by giving more descriptive __h__. You can also use the words __a__, __d__, and __e__ before adjectives and adverbs to add more meaning.

Underline the correct adjective or adverb (in blue) in the sentences below. Then circle the word that the adjective or adverb tells more about.

1. This old (man) was envious/enviously of his pupil's new bagpipes.

2. This boy (walked) proud/proudly off the field.

3. This person communicates happiness through music and a warm/warmly (personality.)

4. This ballerina's Indian name (describes) her life perfect/perfectly.

5. This (person) is famous/famously for composing and performing music.

6. This person (played) the trumpet skillful/skillfully.

7. This ruler brave/bravely (led) his elephants into battle.

8. This character (listened) careful/carefully to the sound of the drums.

9. This boy eager/eagerly (wanted) to learn to make drums "talk."

10. This boy (tried) patient/patiently to teach his new friend everything he knew about drums.

11. These characters (ran) swift/swiftly to win a race.

12. This character brave/bravely (saved) an old woman from the river.

Level 13: Unit 4 Review

Objectives: To describe the relationship between adjectives and adverbs. To select the correct adjective or adverbs to complete sentences. (Language Skills)

91

BEHIND THE SCENES

Read the paragraph below. Then fill in the spaces by circling the letter of the word that best fits the meaning of the paragraph.

The lights dim, the curtain goes up and the play begins! Everything goes so smoothly. Few people are aware of all the work that goes into putting on a play. The actors must learn and rehearse their lines. They have to learn where to stand, move, enter and _____(1)_____ from the stage. Someone must design and make costumes. Another person must plan and apply the actors' make-up. Some people build scenery while other people plan lighting and _____(2)_____ effects such as storms and footsteps on a path. All of this planning and working goes on for weeks, even months, before anyone sees the final play.

1. a. throw   (b.) exit   c. jump

2. (a.) sound   b. musical   c. magical

WHO ARE YOU?

Look back at the picture essay on pages 301-312 ("Time for Fun") and choose a favorite work of art. Complete the chart below about your selection as you did on Workbook page 84.

ART TITLE	Answers will vary.	TIME	
ARTIST		ART FORM	
PLACE		MATERIALS	

Now pretend that you are one of the figures in the picture. On a separate sheet of paper write a paragraph describing who you are and what you are doing. Tell what you see and hear happening around you. Then describe what you are thinking and feeling as the artist has caught you taking "Time for Fun."

Objectives: To organize information. (Study Skills) To use the Cloze procedure to identify missing words using contextual clues.

Similies and Metaphors: Two Kinds of Comparisons

Many storytellers use **similes** (sim′ ə lēz) and **metaphors** (met′ ə fôrz) to add interest and enjoyment to their stories. Both similes and metaphors are forms of comparison that describe one thing in terms of another.

Similes are comparisons that use the words <u>like</u> and <u>as</u>. Find each of the following similes from "The Goldfish" in the story. Then complete the simile by writing its second part on the lines below. Notice how the second part of each simile helps us picture the first part more clearly and dramatically.

This	Is Compared to	This
1. Anemones grew	like	clusters of gay flowers .
2. Great waves rose	like	mountains of glass .
3. The world is	as round as	an orange .
4. He let himself sink	like	a little gold stone .
5. …and silky fins	like	films of moonlit cloud .

Metaphors are comparisons that describe one thing just as if it were the other. A metaphor doesn't say the world is like an orange; it says it is an orange. The little Goldfish unknowingly makes a number of metaphors because he doesn't understand what he sees. See if you can remember what metaphors he makes with each of the following objects. Refer to the story if you need help.

This	Is Said to Be	This
1. The Sun	is	the great Gold Fish .
2. The Moon	is	the great Silver Fish .
3. The Sky	is	blue water .
4. The Ship	is	an enormous fish .
5. The glass globe	is	the whole of the world .

On a separate sheet of paper, choose any five of the above similes and metaphors and complete them with original comparisons of your own. You may enjoy making an illustration for one or more of them.

Level 13: "The Goldfish" pp. 332-341.

Objective: To identify similes and metaphors. (Literary Skill)

93

Reading & Understanding

Like many stories, "The Goldfish" contains elements of both **fact** and **fiction**. While some of the events are **realistic** and based on real-life experiences, others are completely **fantastic** and based only on the author's imagination.

The following sentences give examples of both elements in the story. See if you can identify those events that could happen in real life and those that could only happen in our imaginations. Put an **X** after each event in one of the boxes to show whether you think it should be described as **Realistic** or **Fantastic**.

Story event	Realistic	Fantastic
1. Sometimes the little Goldfish swam down low close to the sand and shell and coral.	X	
2. The little Goldfish thought and talked and felt just like a human being.		X
3. King Neptune warned all of the fish to avoid the net.		X
4. The nearby fishermen spread their nets in the sea.	X	
5. A large ship was becalmed while waiting for the wind to blow.	X	
6. The Ship said, "I am not a fish at all. I am a ship."		X
7. The little Goldfish gasped for air when he leaped out of the water above the waves.	X	
8. The little Goldfish wept for seven days and seven nights because he couldn't reach the Moon.		X
9. King Neptune slipped a second fish in the Fisherman's nets when he wasn't looking.		X
10. The Fisherman put the two little fish in a glass globe with sand and shells and pebbles.	X	

Level 13: "The Goldfish" pp. 332-341.

Objective: To distinguish between realistic and fantastic elements. (Comprehension)

Reading & Remembering

One sign of a good reader is the ability to remember important ideas and details. Let's find out how well you remember what you've read in Eleanor Farjeon's "The Goldfish." Briefly review pages 332-341; then write short answers to the questions below.

A Comprehension Checkup

1. What one thing in the story did King Neptune want all of his "children" to avoid?

   _____the net_____

2. What did the little Goldfish call the Sun? _____the great Gold Fish_____

3. The little Goldfish fell in love with the great Silver Fish. What did the Ship tell him

   it really was? _____the Moon_____

4. What character told the little Goldfish about the world "beyond the rim of things"?

   _____the Ship_____

5. For how long did the little Goldfish weep?_____one week_____

6. Who laughed at the little Goldfish as he lay "swimming in tears"?

   _____the Porpoise_____

7. Who helped the little Goldfish get his wish by telling him to swim to the net?

   _____King Neptune_____

8. What character caught the little Goldfish in his net?_____the Fisherman_____

9. Where did this character place the little Goldfish and his "Silver Bride"?

   _____in a glass bowl or globe_____

10. At last the little Goldfish thought he was greater than the Sun. What did he think

    he had given the little Silverfish?_____"the whole of the world"_____

11. What did King Neptune do as he passed by and listened to the little Goldfish

    bragging? _____He laughed in his beard._____

12. Can you finish these last words of King Neptune? "It was a shame to let such a tiny

    fellow loose in the vast ocean. He needed a world more suited to his_____size_____."

USING THE CONTEXT

Read the paragraphs below. Using the context, decide on the meaning of the underlined word. Circle the letter of the correct meaning.

1. The two Buzzards listened to the Snake and felt sorry for him . . . They tried to make this Snake more accepting of his <u>lot</u>.

   (a.) situation   b. looks   c. home

2. "Aha, yes," sighed the Snake, "but I am <u>at heart</u> like you two. Deep inside, I am really a bird."

   a. in love   b. in pain   (c.) in feeling

3. The two Buzzards drew closer together on the stone. . . . They began to think very <u>hard</u>.

   (a.) carefully   b. quickly   c. heavily

4. Wait! There is one way we can take you for a little *paseo* into the sky.

   (a.) walk   b. money   c. lightning

5. So the two birds went nearby on the desert and brought back a dried-up yucca <u>stalk</u>.

   a. flower   (b.) stick   c. tree

6. The breath was knocked out of him, and <u>countless</u> cactus thorns were knocked into him by his fall.

   (a.) many   b. sharp   c. strange

7. Soon he gathered himself together and crawled back to his <u>den</u> in the rocks.

   a. stone   (b.) home   c. dent

8. The Ship said to the Goldfish: "My little friend, if you were the Moon <u>yonder</u> . . . you could only see one half of these things at a time."

   a. golden   (b.) out there   c. spirit

9. The things the Ship had told him about were more than he could understand, but they filled him with great <u>longings</u>—longings to possess the Silver Moon and to be a mightier fish than the Sun. . . ."

   a. headaches   (b.) desires   c. jokes

10. Peering through the branches of the coral tree, he beheld a plump Porpoise bursting its sides with laughter. . . . He stopped to ask the Porpoise, "What <u>tickles</u> you so?"

    a. scratches   b. hurts   (c.) amuses

11. The Ship said: "Just now I am doing nothing, for I am <u>becalmed.</u> But when the wind blows, I shall go sailing around the world."

    a. sunk   b. sitting and thinking   (c.) motionless without wind

12. "A tiny fellow like you can never hope to see more than a <u>scrap</u> of the world."

    (a.) little piece   b. garbage   c. bottom

13. He swam boldly to the net which was waiting to catch what it could. As the <u>meshes</u> closed upon the Goldfish. . .

    (a.) cords of a net.   b. hooks
    c. bravery

14. The Fisherman bought a globe of glass and sprinkled sand and shells and tiny pebbles at the bottom. He set among them a <u>sprig</u> of coral.

    a. huge piece   (b.) small piece
    c. crushed piece

Level 13: "The Snake Who Wanted to Fly" pp. 344-349.

Objective: To use context clues to determine the meaning of story words. (Comprehension)

Identifying Characters and Drawing Conclusions

Read the sentences in each item and then answer the questions. You may wish to use some of the words in the left-hand column in your answers.

1. "How lucky you two are. You can travel through the air. I must always go with my stomach to the ground. . . . I am at heart like you two. Deep inside I am really a bird. That is what I am."

Who said this? _____ the Snake _____

How would you describe someone who talks like this?
_____ complaining, envious, unrealistic, foolish, etc. _____

2. "Flying seems pleasant enough . . . but we are no closer to the blue sky than you are here on the ground. . . . Wait, there is one way we can take you for a little *paseo* into the sky. We will carry you . . . that is what we'll do!"

Who said this? _____ the Buzzards _____

How would you describe these speakers? _____ honest, _____
_____ realistic, generous, clever, cooperative, etc. _____

3. "Flap your wings, Brother Snake," he said. "Do I see feathers growing at your tail?"

Who said this? _____ the Eagle _____

How would you describe this character? _____ mean, _____
_____ sarcastic, unkind, insulting, etc. _____

4. "Don't answer him. He is trying to make you talk and open your mouth. If you did that, you would lose your hold on the stick and fall to the ground."

Who said this? _____ the dove _____

What do these words show about the character? _____
_____ She's kind, generous, intelligent, logical, etc. _____

5. When this character had a little experience with flying, he "seemed to think that he knew all about it." Seeing the Dove so close to him, he forgot he was "not a bird and opened his jaws to make a grab for the Dove."

Who behaved like this? _____ the Snake _____

How would you describe these actions? _____
_____ greedy, mean, unfair, foolish, etc. _____

On a separate sheet of paper write a few sentences about each of the major characters. (Describe the Buzzards together.) Tell which ones you admire and which ones you do not admire. Explain your judgments in terms of the character's behavior.

clever

foolish

kind

mean

generous

greedy

complaining

honest

logical

cooperative

envious

realistic

unrealistic

intelligent

sarcastic

unfair

Level 13: "The Snake Who Wanted to Fly" pp. 344-349.

Objective: To draw conclusions about the details in a selection. (Comprehension)

WORDS and WORD PARTS

Here are eight compound words. Compound words have two or more base words joined together. Draw a line between the two base words in each compound. Then write each base word in the chart below.

anything	nearby	understand	goldfish
nowhere	downfall	overhead	handkerchief

A **base word** is a word that may stand alone or be joined to other words or word parts.

An **affix** is a word part that cannot stand alone; it must be joined to other word parts.

WORD PATTERN: COMPOUND

Base	+	Base
any		thing
no		where
near		by
down		fall
under		stand
over		head
gold		fish
hand		kerchief

Here are ten more words. Each word contains a base and one affix. Underline the base of each word. Then write the base and its affix in the right columns below. Remember that an affix that comes before a base word is called a prefix; an affix that comes after a base word is called a suffix.

darkness	friendship	impossible	reteach	tasteful
countless	unhappy	distrust	arrangement	midnight

WORD PATTERN: BASE + AFFIXES

Prefix	+	Base		Base	+	Suffix
im		possible		dark		ness
re		teach		friend		ship
un		happy		taste		ful
dis		trust		count		less
mid		night		arrange		ment

Level 13: "The Snake Who Wanted to Fly" pp. 344-349.

Objective: To distinguish base words from affixes and other base words as a means for dividing between syllables. (Language Skills)

Cause and Effect: Or How One Thing Leads to Another

What caused each event listed below from "Anansi's Hat-Shaking Dance" to happen? Write the number of each story event that is an effect next to the event that caused it.

STORY EFFECTS

1. Anansi attended a family funeral.
2. He became terribly hungry.
3. He tried to steal a spoonful of beans.
4. He invented the story of the "hat-shaking dance."
5. He leaped into the tall grass.

STORY CAUSES

3	Anansi became terribly hungry
5	Anansi was overcome with shame
1	Anansi's mother-in-law died
4	Anansi couldn't admit the truth
2	Anansi tried to fast for eight days

So far in this unit, you have read three folktales. Their titles are listed below.

1. "The Goldfish"   2. "The Snake Who Wanted to Fly"
3. "Anansi's Hat-Shaking Dance

The following moral lessons may be matched with the three animal stories in "A World of Wonders." Write the story number in front of the sentence that best describes the lesson learned by each story's main character.

Three Moral Lessons

2   Discontent and greed often lead to disaster.

3   Vanity and dishonesty often lead to shame.

1   Ignorance and inexperience often lead to sadness.

Match the following animal characters with each of the folktales in Unit 5. Write the story number in front of each animal. Two animals are listed for each folktale.

Six Animal Characters

2	eagle	1	porpoise	1	silverfish
3	rabbit	3	guinea fowl	2	dove

Objectives: To identify cause and effect relationships in a story. To identify the theme of a selection. To identify characters from a selection. (Comprehension)

WHEN, WHAT and WHY?

The pictures below are from "Anansi's Hat-Shaking Dance," but they are not in the correct order. Number the events to show the order in which they took place in the story. Now write a few sentences on the lines next to each picture to tell what Anansi was doing in that part of the story. Also tell why the rabbit and the other animals were looking at him as they did. If you need more space, use a separate sheet of paper.

The animals are looking amazed, even scared, as Anansi does his wild "hat-shaking dance." Actually, Anansi is hiding hot beans under his hat. He was going to eat the beans but the other animals came to see him.

2

Anansi has torn the hat from his head because of the terrible heat of the hot beans. The other animals laugh and jeer at Anansi when they find out why he has been dancing so wildly. Anansi jumps into the tall grasses to hide in shame.

3

Anansi is telling how sad he is about his mother-in-law's death. He is saying that he will go for eight days without eating to show his respect for her. The animals look puzzled, sad and a bit suspicious, knowing that Anansi can be quite a show-off.

1

Level 13: "Anansi's Hat-Shaking Dance" pp. 350-355.
Objective: To order events in the correct sequence. (Comprehension)

Here is a review of three simple rules for dividing many words with bases and affixes of one syllable. Read the rules and complete the following exercise.

SAMPLE WORDS

<u>some</u>one	<u>great</u>est
dis<u>trust</u>	<u>scarecrow</u>
<u>near</u>by	pre<u>judge</u>
<u>shout</u>ing	re<u>call</u>ing
<u>outdone</u>	un<u>know</u>ingly

1.

The first step in dividing a word into syllables is to find its **base.** Underline the base part in each of the words in the box at the right. Remember that some words may have more than one base.

2.

There are four **compound words** in the box above. Find the words and write the **two bases** of each compound word in the boxes at the right. As you divide the bases, you are also dividing each word into its **two syllables.**

BASE	+	BASE
some		one
scare		crow
near		by
out		done

3.

If word **affixes** are also of one syllable, we may separate the base from the affixes and often produce the correct syllabication pattern. Here are four different **word patterns.** See if you can find words from the SAMPLE WORDS above to fit each pattern. Write the bases and affixes for each word in the appropriate boxes.

a.

PREFIX	+	BASE
dis		trust
pre		judge

b.

BASE	+	SUFFIX
shout		ing
great		est

c.

PREFIX	+	BASE	+	SUFFIX
re		call		ing

d.

PREFIX	+	BASE	+	SUFFIX	+	SUFFIX
un		know		ing		ly

WORDS and WORD PARTS

Objective: To describe the rules for syllabicating words composed of a base word and an affix of one syllable. (Decoding/Encoding Skills)

DESCRIPTIVE ADJECTIVES

Some adjectives from "Too Much Nose" are written in the box. The nouns that these adjectives describe in the story are listed below. Write each adjective in front of the noun described on the listed page. Then write nouns of your own that might be described by the same adjectives.

| ripe | wonderful | too much | terrible | mysterious |
| angry | shiny, silver | rusty | broken | ragged |

page		story adjectives	story nouns	your nouns
362	1.	shiny, silver	coin	shield
364	2.	ragged	purse	Answers will vary.
369	3.	wonderful	medicine	
367	4.	ripe	figs	
365	5.	mysterious	voice	
359	6.	broken	hat	
368	7.	terrible	fuss	
370	8.	angry	queen	
359	9.	rusty	horn	
368	10.	too much	nose	

Match the following adjective synonyms. Write the letter of the word on the left in front of its synonym on the right.

Adjectives	Synonyms	Adjectives	Synonyms
a. ragged	_f_ marvelous	a. huge	_e_ bent
b. mysterious	_b_ unknown	b. timid	_c_ full
c. angry	_d_ crushed	c. stuffed	_b_ shy
d. broken	_e_ awful	d. scrawny	_f_ special
e. terrible	_a_ shabby	e. crooked	_d_ skinny
f. wonderful	_c_ furious	f. extraordinary	_a_ enormous

Level 13: "Too Much Nose" pp. 358-371.
Objectives: To explore author's use of language. (Comprehension) To locate adjectives that describe story nouns. (Language Skills)

TESTING YOUR MEMORY

See how many details you remember about the plot and characters in "Too Much Nose." Read the following sentences. Then underline the word or words in blue that best complete each sentence. You may wish to skim quickly through the story before you begin.

1. The very poor and very old father took his sons' three gifts from a   cabinet—closet—chest.

2. The second son received a   coin purse—horn—hat.

3. Each of the sons was   delighted—disappointed—amused   with his gift.

4. A palace maid asked the second son to come in and play   chess—cards—checkers   with the queen.

5. The queen won   three—thirteen—thirty   pieces of silver in her game with the second son.

6. Shortly after, the second son returned to the palace; but this time the queen didn't recognize him because he was wearing   his brother's hat—a beard—a long nose.

7. After the queen had outsmarted the second son a second time, he made a third trip to the castle and produced   a basket of cherries—an army—thirty silver coins.

8. Now that the second son had lost everything, he began wandering until he fell asleep under a magic   pear—cherry—fig   tree.

9. He ate the magic fruit, and his nose grew longer and longer. Luckily, he came across another magic tree covered with   cherries—pears—figs.

10. When no one could cure long noses in the queen's palace, the second son disguised himself as a   peddler—doctor—professor.

11. At last, the second son was able to trick the queen by appealing to her weakness for   eating cherries—showing-off—playing cards.

12. The second son got out of the castle without being caught because he was   running so fast—disguised with a beard—invisible.

Level 13: "Too Much Nose" pp. 358–371.

Objective: To identify story details of plot and character. (Comprehension)

A VARIETY OF VERBS

Find each story verb below on the listed page. Decide which of the two verbs that follow is closer in meaning and underline the correct one. Then underline the words on the right which tell how the story verbs and its synonyms are alike.

	Story Verb	Page	Closer Synonym	Because Both Verbs Suggest . . .	
1.	exclaimed	359	whispered or <u>cried out</u>	<u>excitement</u>	boredom
2.	snatched	364	eased or <u>grabbed</u>	slow action	<u>sudden action</u>
3.	begged	365	<u>pleaded</u> or requested	politeness	<u>earnestness</u>
4.	grumble	365	shriek or <u>mutter</u>	loud anger	<u>quiet anger</u>
5.	cried	365	<u>shouted</u> or said	<u>loud voices</u>	soft voices
6.	batter	366	<u>knock down</u> or rearrange	<u>forcefulness</u>	peacefulness
7.	feasted	368	nibbled or <u>gorged</u>	<u>eating a lot</u>	eating a little
8.	boast	369	announce or <u>brag</u>	<u>acting proud</u>	acting ashamed
9.	flipped	370	<u>tossed</u> or arranged	slowness	<u>quickness</u>
10.	vanished	370	left or <u>disappeared</u>	<u>suddenness</u>	leisure

---

Which verbs on the left would be used if you wanted to indicate the following kinds of walking? Can you think of any others? Use a dictionary if you need help.

Other possibilities:

tiptoe	1. walk with a regular rhythm <u>march</u>	<u>pace, etc.</u>
march	2. walk with a tired and heavy step <u>plod</u>	<u>trudge, tramp, etc.</u>
stroll	3. walk delicately <u>tiptoe</u>	<u>glide, prance, etc.</u>
plod	4. walk rapidly <u>scurry</u>	<u>scamper, etc.</u>
strut	5. walk proudly <u>strut</u>	<u>swagger</u>
stomp	6. walk with an angry step <u>stomp</u>	<u>stalk, march, etc.</u>
scurry	7. walk for pleasure <u>stroll</u>	<u>amble, saunter, etc.</u>

Level 13: "Too Much Nose" pp. 358-371.

Objectives: To identify the precise meanings of verbs that describe action in a selection. To supply colorful verbs to describe actions in a selection. (Comprehension)

NEW STORY WORDS

STORY SYNONYMS

Write the letters of the words in the first box in front of the words with the closest meanings in the second box.

a. mumble	b. tumbledown	c. sprightly	d. weary
e. prodigious	f. moan	g. bedazzled	h. unbelievable

__b__ ramshackle	__g__ awestruck	__f__ groan	__c__ lively
__h__ incredible	__d__ tired	__e__ great	__a__ mutter

MOUNTAIN TALK

The kingdom in "The Patchwork Princess" is way far back in the hill country, and the characters use many folksy words. Find story words on the pages given that match the definitions below. Write the word you find.

page

372   a word for worry __fret__

372   a word for pieces of material

      sewn together __patchwork__

373   relatives __kinfolk__

page

372   a name for Father __Pappy__

374   a violin __fiddle__

374   a word for a violin player __fiddler__

375   a group of people __clan__

ROYAL WORDS

Because our story is also about people who live in a kingdom, there are also many "royal words." See if you can find these words and write them on the lines below.

page

376   the land ruled

      by a king __kingdom__

375   a metal suit worn

      for protection __armor__

375   an object carried with a sword for

      protection __shield__

page

372   a king's home __castle__

372   a large formal dance __ball__

372   a long formal dress __gown__

376   a delicate and light cloth __gossamer__

376   royal head gear __crown__

Objective: To explore the author's use of words in a selection. (Comprehension)

PRIME RHYME TIME

Answer the questions below by writing the letter of the correct answer in the blank on the right.

1. Which of the following phrases from "The Patchwork Princess" is an example of rhyme? _c_

    a. Prodigious, Portentous, Phenomenal

    b. With a bit of lace and a speck of trim. . .

    c. Cobbler, Gobbler, Hobbler

2. Do rhyming words have the same **a.** beginning **b.** middle **c.** end sounds? _c_

3. Do we find rhyming words more frequently in

    a. stories   **b.** poems   **c.** biographies? _b_

4. Which of these characters in the story use rhyming words? _c_

    a. The king and the kinfolk   **b.** Rosybell and the Prince   **c.** The king and Rosybell

5. When does the king use rhyming words? _a_

    a. Usually when he is in trouble and wants something.

    b. When he is trying to cheer everyone up.

    c. He never uses them.

6. When does Rosybell use rhyming words? _b_

    a. When she is trying to help her father remember the magic words.

    b. When she is helping solve the people's problems.

    c. She never uses them.

7. Complete the king's rhyming phrases by writing the number of the correct missing word in the blank.

    a. soggy, foggy, _2_   1. grand

    b. moan, groan, _3_   2. boggy

    c. land, sand _1_   3. drone

8. Match the letters of the king's words above with the problems he wanted solved.

    _b_   Night came and everyone on the raft was very sad.

    _c_   The raft floated to land.

    _a_   The rains had flooded the kingdom.

Level 13: "The Patchwork Princess" pp. 372-377.

Objectives: To recognize rhyme as literary device. (Literary Skill) To supply rhymes related to story events. (Comprehension)

9. Write the rhyming word that Rosybell used to go with each of the sentences below.

a. We need a craft. Let's build a ___raft___.

b. Let's take a chance and have that ___dance___.

c. We can make a sail and catch this ___gale___.

10. Match the letters of Rosybell's rhyming words in 9 with the way she solved the people's problems below.

___c___ Rosybell helped the raft reach dry land.

___a___ Rosybell helped the people escape from the flood.

___b___ Rosybell helped cheer the people when they were sad and frightened.

11. What was funny about the king's three magic ''rhyming words'' when he finally remembered them? ___c___

a. They had been written on the moonstone all the time.

b. He had come very close to saying them several times.

c. They weren't rhyming words at all.

12. What rhyming words might the king choose if these events happened? Write the most likely rhyming word to complete each statement.

a. ''The raft has sunk. Oh mad, bad, ___sad___.''

       sad   **glad**   **cry**

b. ''Ah, listen to the birds in this fine land. Oh, wing, ring, ___sing___.''

       string   **fly**   **sing**

c. ''Ring the chimes for Rosybell's wedding! Oh, tell, well, ___bell___.''

       gong   **bell**   **sell**

13. Now think up something that might happen to the king when he returns to his castle. Write three rhyming words that he would use to tell about the event.

Event: ___Answers will vary.___

_____

Rhyming words: _____

_____

WORD MEANING IN SENTENCE CONTEXT

Read the following sentences. Then decide which of the words that follow are closest in meaning to the underlined word in the sentence. Underline the best synonym.

Sentences	Synonyms		
1. After their parents went out, the children plotted the details of the surprise party.	planned	dreamed	forgot
2. The acorn-sized doll was in a wee blue pretty box.	pretty	heavy	tiny
3. I need a large bucket right away. Will you fetch it for me?	fill	get	paint
4. The girl closed her door to shut out the din of her brother's piano playing, her mother's vacuuming, and the dog's barking.	music	rhythm	noise
5. The scouts could see where the foxes roamed by their tracks in the snow.	walked	sleep	eat
6. Rip Van Winkle was feeling a bit sleepy so he decided to doze for a while.	time	rest	nap
7. The swimmers shuddered when they first felt the icy water on their feet.	dived	raced	shook
8. After making fifteen pies, twenty cakes, and forty dozen biscuits, the baker said she was too exhausted to make a batch of cookies.	busy	tired	worried
9. The back-hill people were completely dismayed by the sudden flooding of the kingdom.	troubled	angry	bored
10. The children and their teacher made a bargain that for every perfect spelling score the teacher would read an extra page of their favorite story.	argument	appointment	agreement
11. The ship drifted slowly in the breeze.	moved	raced	sank
12. The woman had no notion of staying in fairyland.	fear	idea	picture
13. The tiny teacup was very dainty.	full	heavy	delicate
14. The baker's husband was all in a whirl from the strange happenings.	confused state	wheel	wing
15. The baker swished the batter with her spoon.	tasted	mixed	baked

Choose five underlined words above and use them in five original sentences.

Level 13: "The Woman Who Flummoxed the Fairies" pp. 378-387.

Objective: To use context clues to determine the meaning of words. (Comprehension)

People who speak the same language may speak different variations of that language or different **dialects.** Here are some words from ''The Patchwork Princess'' and ''The Woman Who Flummoxed the Fairies'' that are from two different dialects of English. Match the words in Column A with their definitions in Column B.

HOW DO YOU SAY IT?

Column A

_e_ kinfolk

_a_ fret

_b_ fetch

_f_ wee

_c_ babe

_d_ clan

Column B

a. worry

b. bring

c. infant

d. group of people joined
   together in some way

e. relatives

f. little

Here are words from different dialects in the United States. Look at the words after each number in Column A. Underline the word you would be most likely to use. Then match that group of words with the correct definition in Column B.

Column A

1. brook, creek, run, branch

2. mud worm, night crawler,
   angleworm, fish worm

3. bag, sack, tote, poke

4. pail, bucket

5. hero, grinder, submarine

Column B

_2_ **a.** earthworm

_5_ **b.** sandwich made from a
   long loaf of bread

_1_ **c.** running stream

_3_ **d.** paper container

_4_ **e.** round container for carrying
   liquids

Now rewrite these sentences using words in your dialect.

1. 'Twas plain to see that the wee babe was unhappy. Possible answers:
   It was clear that the little baby was unhappy.

2. Don't fret; maybe your kinfolk can help you.
   Don't worry; maybe your relatives can help you.

3. The bucket is in that creek. _____ Answers will vary. _____

4. What's in that poke? A grinder? _____

5. Howdy! How ya doin'? _____

WORD DETECTIVE

What words do you think are missing from the sentences in this story? Fill in the blanks with words that make the best sense for each sentence.

Once there were three bears who lived in a _____little_____ house in the woods. There was a mother bear, _____a_____ father bear, and a baby bear. One beautiful fall _____day_____ the bear family decided to walk through the woods.

_____While_____ they were gone, a little girl named Gingeremma walked _____past_____ their house. She was very tired so she went _____inside_____ to rest. She tried the first two beds but _____they_____ were too large and uncomfortable. Then she tried the _____small_____ bed but it was so small her feet hung _____over_____ the edge. Poor Gingeremma. What bad luck!

Next she looked in the dining room where mother bear had left _____some_____ hot cereal to cool. Gingeremma was hungry, so she _____tasted_____ it. It was terrible! Not enough honey. Poor Gingeremma. _____What_____ bad luck!

Gingeremma decided to head for home. She _____couldn't_____ wait to get there. Her furniture was just the right _____size_____ and her food was just the way she liked _____it_____. As she disappeared into the woods, the bear family _____returned_____ home from their walk. It was a lucky day _____for_____ Gingeremma after all!

Level 13: "The Woman Who Flummoxed the Fairies" pp. 378-387.

Objective: To provide practice with the Cloze procedure. To identify missing words using contextual and grammatic clues. (Comprehension)

WHEN MAGIC CHANGES YOUNG TO OLD

There are a number of funny moments in "A Tale of Stolen Time" that occur because four children have been transformed into **looking** but not always **acting** like very old people. Here are six pairs of events from the story. In each pair one event has characters acting in the way we would **expect** them to act. The other event, due to the magic which changes young to old, has people behaving in such unexpected ways that we have to laugh. After you have read the two events in each pair, put an X in front of the event that has people acting in a surprising, funny, and unexpected manner.

1. _____ a. Peter's mother hears the doorbell and goes to answer the door.
   __X__ b. Peter's mother opens the door, looks at her son, and says, "Whom do you want to see, sir?"

2. __X__ a. Peter begins to cry and wipes his tears with his long beard.
   _____ b. Peter cries because he is very sad and lonely.

3. _____ a. Peter meets an old lady on the street and calls her Granny.
   __X__ b. Peter asks the old lady if she is in the fourth grade.

4. _____ a. Peter finds a little old woman sitting on a park bench.
   __X__ b. The little old woman is playing with a ball and tossing away the raisins in her bread.

5. __X__ a. Peter and Maria find another old lady playing hopscotch.
   _____ b. The old lady is in the backyard of her home.

6. _____ a. At last Maria spots an old man riding on a trolley.
   __X__ b. The old man's hat is pulled over one ear, his beard is waving in the wind, and he is whistling as he rides along.

Level 13: "A Tale of Stolen Time" pp. 392-407.

Objective: To identify story events with humorous incongruities. (Comprehension)

111

Words for Young and Old

The contrast of youth and age plays an important part in many fairy tales. In the Word Box, eight words are associated with the **young** people in the story, and eight words are associated with the story's **old** people. Read the words through once silently; then write each of the words under its appropriate heading below.

Word Box

beard	growing up	sighing	boy
ball	grown-up	skipping	grandfather
hopscotch	groaning	homework	granny
hobbling	giggling	wrinkles	girl

From "A Tale of Stolen Time"

Words for the Young	Words for the Old
ball	beard
hopscotch	hobbling
growing up	grown-up
giggling	groaning
skipping	sighing
homework	wrinkles
boy	grandfather
girl	granny

Level 13: "A Tale of Stolen Time" pp. 392-407.

Objective: To classify words into contrasting categories of meaning. (Comprehension)

Which Will Win–Good or Evil?

In fairy tales, good and evil forces often struggle to gain control of the main characters. Here are four examples of these opposite forces from the last four tales in Unit 5. Write the number of the story in front of the example that best describes the story's elements of good and evil.

1. "Too Much Nose"
2. "The Patchwork Princess"
3. "The Woman Who Flummoxed the Fairies"
4. "A Tale of Stolen Time"

Story	Good	Evil
2	cheerfulness optimism hard work	giving up poverty and flood idleness
4	efficiency using time wisely hard work	laziness wasting time using time foolishly
3	cheerfulness cleverness soft-heartedness	selfishness capturing people complaining
1	honesty trust kindness	dishonesty scheming wickedness

Words That Mean Almost the Same Thing

Read the list of words below. Then read the sentences. Find a synonym in the list for each underlined word. Then write the letter of that synonym in the blank before the sentence.

a. muttering   **b.** whitish   **c.** rough

d. saw   **e.** not moving   **f.** soft

_c_ 1. Why is your voice so hoarse today?

_b_ 2. He had turned into a thin, pale old man.

_f_ 3. In a faint whisper, Peter spoke to his mother.

_d_ 4. Just then he spied a tiny white house.

_a_ 5. The children were sighing and mumbling.

_e_ 6. If the children touch the clock, we will be motionless.

Level 13: "A Tale of Stolen Time" pp. 392–407.

Objectives: To identify the conflict between good and evil as a characteristic of the fairy tale. (Literary Skill) To use context clues to expand word meaning. (Comprehension)

113

Classifying the Classics

In the unit entitled "A World of Wonders," we have read seven tales from around the world. The titles and page numbers of our seven stories are listed in the box below.

1. "The Goldfish," pages 332–341
2. "The Snake Who Wanted to Fly," pages 344–349
3. "Anansi's Hat-Shaking Dance," pages 350–355
4. "Too Much Nose," pages 358–371
5. "The Patchwork Princess," pages 372–377
6. "The Woman Who Flummoxed the Fairies," pages 378-387
7. "A Tale of Stolen Time," pages 392-407

Underline the word or words in blue that correctly complete the sentences below.

1. **Fiction writing** is about   informative— imaginary   people and happenings.
2. Many— All   of the stories in Unit 5 are fiction.
3. Fiction writing may be **realistic** and true-to-life, or exaggerated and **fantastic.** The story events in the unit "A World of Wonders" may be described as largely   realistic— fantastic.

Here are some imaginary people and events from each of the seven stories in Unit 5. Match each story with its parts of make-believe by writing the story's number in the blank.

_4_   A hat that makes its wearer invisible

_2_   Two talking buzzards

_7_   Four children who are changed into old people

_1_   A sea god who looks after all of his underwater children

_3_   A spider with a full head of hair

_6_   A baker finds herself in fairyland

_5_   A king who has forgotten some magic words

Objectives: Classifying stories into various categories of literary genre. (Literary Skill) To recall details of plot and setting from selections. (Comprehension)

Complete the following statements by underlining the correct word or words that are printed in blue.

FOLK TALE

1. A **folk tale** is a story or legend that has been invented and passed on by   one storyteller—<u>many storytellers.</u>
2. Folk tales usually have   one version—<u>many versions.</u>
3. Most folk tales were   <u>told before they were written</u>—written before they were told.
4. A common beginning word for folk tales is   "Now"—<u>"Once".</u>
5. Folk tales come from countries   <u>all over the world</u>—in Europe and Asia.

The following countries represent the story settings of six folk tales in Unit 5. Write the numbers of the stories on the blanks in front of the story settings.

Six Story Settings

__4__ Italy   __3__ Ghana   __1__ Japan

__7__ Russia   __6__ Scotland   __2__ Mexico

Underline the word or words in blue that correctly complete the following statements.

FAIRY TALE

1. A **fairy tale** is a kind of folk tale that **may** have fairies, but **must** have   monsters—<u>magic.</u>
2. The **main characters** in fairy tales are usually   <u>ordinary</u>—extraordinary   people whose lives are suddenly transformed by   ordinary—<u>extraordinary</u>   events.
3. **The plot** of many fairy tales involves a **moral struggle** with the forces of **good** finally   <u>overcoming</u>—losing   to the forces of **evil**.
4. The   first—<u>last</u>   four   tales   in   "A   World   of   Wonders"   may be classified as fairy tales.

Here are six sources of magic in the four fairy tales in Unit 5. Write the number of the story in front of each magical object or being.

Magical Objects and Beings

__6__ fairy dust   __5__ three magic words

__4__ a rusty horn   __7__ a tiny white house

__7__ a wind up clock   __4__ a ripe cherry tree

Sounds and Syllables

When bases or affixes have more than one syllable, we may use the following rules to help us determine where to divide between the syllables in order to achieve **correct pronunciation.**

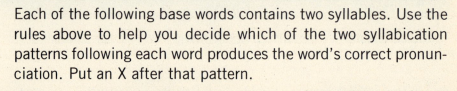

> **a. Separate between two unlike consonant letters.**
>
>   **Examples:**   cer/ tain   win/ dow
>
> **b. Do not separate between two letters that stand for one sound.**
>
>   **Examples:**   Double Consonants   Consonant Digraphs
>   as in: butt/ er   nick/ el
>
> **c. Separate before a single consonant letter if the preceding vowel is pronounced long. Examples:**   no/ tice   ti/ ny
>   **Separate after a single consonant letter if the preceding vowel is pronounced short.** Examples: nov/ el   tim/ id
>
> **d. Do not separate between consonants that form sound clusters such as, br, cl, gr, pl, st, str, etc.**
>
>   **Examples:**   in/ stinct   com/ plete

Each of the following base words contains two syllables. Use the rules above to help you decide which of the two syllabication patterns following each word produces the word's correct pronunciation. Put an X after that pattern.

1. circus
cir cus___X___
circ us_____

2. buzzard
buz zard_____
buzz ard _X_

3. pocket
poc ket_____
pock et__X__

4. moment
mom ent_____
mo ment__X__

5. follow
fol low_____
foll ow__X__

6. purchase
pur chase__X__
purc hase_____

7. gentle
gen tle__X__
gent le_____

8. doctor
doc tor __X__
doct or _____

9. table
tab le_____
ta ble__X__

10. journey
jour ney__X__
journ ey_____

11. magic
mag ic__X__
ma gic_____

12. enough
en ough_____
e nough__X__

Objective: To identify and describe syllabication patterns for word parts of two or more syllables. (Decoding/Encoding Skills)

ACTION-PAST AND PRESENT

Regular verbs add -ed to their present form to show that something happened in the past.

    Today I talk.   Yesterday I talked.

Irregular verbs have special words to show that something happened in the past.

    Today I eat.   Yesterday I ate.

Write the correct past form of the verbs on the left to complete the sentences.

1. bring   The fairies _____ brought _____ the husband to fairyland.

2. laugh   King Neptune _____ laughed _____ in his beard.

3. find   The little Goldfish _____ found _____ happiness in the glass globe.

4. has   The second son _____ had _____ all three gifts.

5. go   Anansi _____ went _____ into the tall grass quickly.

6. stand   Rosybell _____ stood _____ up in the middle of the raft.

Tell Me A Story...

Read the paragraph below. Then fill in the spaces by circling the letter of the word that best fits the meaning of the paragraph.

    Many stories we enjoy reading today are very old. No one knows exactly how all these stories were started. Most likely many of the stories were made up to explain events in nature that people did not _____ **(1)** _____. These stories often used magic or people with special powers to explain events such as why it rains or why it grows dark at night. Other stories were made up to warn people of things that would happen to people who were bad. These stories told about the bad things that would happen to people who were lazy, _____ **(2)** _____, or who mistreated others.

    Much later these stories were written down, not to warn or explain, but to be enjoyed.

1. a. know about   b. like   c. understand   d. care for

2. a. happy   b. greedy   c. pleasant   d. kind

Objective: To supply the past form of regular and irregular verbs. (Language Skills) To use the Cloze procedure to identify missing words using contextual clues.(Comprehension)

CAN YOU READ A MAP?

A **map** is a drawing of an area. It shows the area as it would look from above. A map gives information about where places are; how far they are from each other; their size; the location of rivers, mountains, and oceans; and much more.

The map below shows the country where Cecile and her parents live. The **compass** next to the map shows the four directions. The **map legend** tells you what the symbols on the map mean. Read the map and answer the questions that follow.

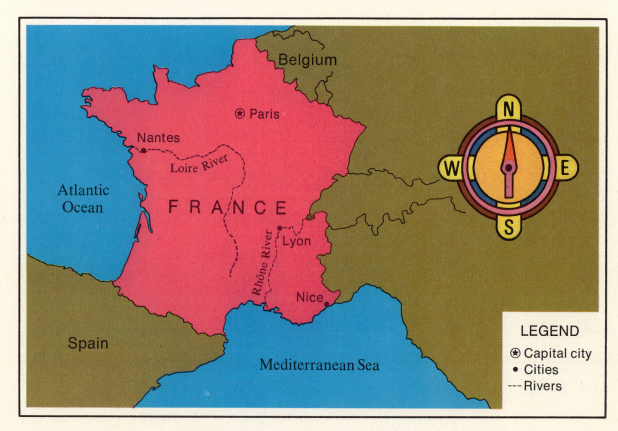

LEGEND
⊛ Capital city
• Cities
--- Rivers

1. In what country do the Durands live? __France__
2. Find the city they live in, Nice. On what sea is it located?
   __Mediterranean Sea__
3. What city is the capital of France? __Paris__
4. Find Paris. Circle the direction that Cecile would travel to go from Nice to Paris.

   (northwest)   south   east
5. What country lies south of France? __Spain__
6. Circle the ways Cecile could travel from Nice to Paris.

   (automobile)   (airplane)   boat
7. Name a city between Nice and Paris. __Lyon__
8. If traveling on land from Nice to Paris, what river would have to be crossed? ___
   __Rhône River__

Level 13: "The Day Jean-Pierre Went Round the World" pp. 414-428.

Objective: To use a map to find specific geographical locations. (Study Skill)

Reading Between the Lines

Read and follow the instructions given for each item below. Write the letter of your answer on the line at the left of each question.

___a___ **1.** Reread page 415 beginning with "There had been great excitement. . . ." The author, Paul Gallico, never directly describes the "suitable box" to the reader. What do you think the box is supposed to be used for?
   a. to hold Jean-Pierre   **b.** to hold Jean-Pierre's food supplies
   c. to hold Jean-Pierre's gift for Aunt Louise

___a___ **2.** Reread the first paragraph on page 418 under the subtitle "A Surprise from Thailand." Although Mr. Gallico doesn't tell us how Cecile feels, he gives us many clues to her state of mind. Which of these words best describes her emotions at this time?
   a. nervous and worried   **b.** relaxed and happy   **c.** tired and sleepy

___b___ **3.** On page 419, Cecile gets a letter. Read the paragraph that starts "Cecile took it and ran to her. . . ." What did Cecile mean when she said the letter was "funny-looking"?
   a. it was out of shape   **b.** it had unusual stamps and new handwriting
   c. there was a joke on the envelope.

___b___ **4.** Reread the second paragraph on page 423 beginning with, "For a moment . . ." When Cecile hears Jean-Pierre's chirrups, teeth clicking, and sneezes she should feel—
   a. scared because it's a sign he's catching a cold.   **b.** happy because Jean-Pierre is excited and probably recognizes her voice.   **c.** annoyed because it shows he isn't paying attention to her.

___b___ **5.** Reread the first two paragraphs on page 425 beginning with, "Hurried phone calls. . . ." We aren't told what happens over the next five days. Which of the following explanations do you think is most likely?
   a. The professor is probably performing experiments on Jean-Pierre in his laboratory.   **b.** The professor is probably giving Jean-Pierre medicine and helping nurse him back to health.   **c.** Jean-Pierre has probably been misplaced again and it takes that long for the professor to find him.

___b___ **6.** Reread page 426. By the preparation that has been made for Jean-Pierre's arrival, we can tell that by now this little guinea pig is—
   a. being taken very seriously.   **b.** looked at as just another lost pet.
   c. obviously mistaken for somebody else.

Level 13: "The Day Jean-Pierre Went Round the World" pp. 414-428.   **119**

Objective: To make inferences from information given. (Comprehension)

Major and Minor Characters

Sometimes story characters are described by the terms **major** and **minor**. Here are seven characters from Paul Gallico's "The Day Jean-Pierre Went Round the World." Complete the exercise below and decide how each of these characters should be classified.

Aunt Louise	**Cecile**	**Professor Jones**
Sirima Desjardins	**Jean-Pierre** **Y.A. Chin**	**Flippo, the Clown**

Major characters are the main characters in the action of the plot. The story's theme centers on them. What two characters in "The Day Jean-Pierre Went Round the World" might be called the major characters? Circle their names in the box above.

Minor characters do not play a central role in a story. Instead, they appear in the background of events. They are usually seen and heard less than the major characters. Which minor character answers each of the following descriptions?

1. What character had "educated kangaroos and trained pigs"?

   Flippo, the clown

2. What character let Jean-Pierre "make a pig of himself" by eating unusual Hawaiian foods?

   Y. A. Chin

3. Who cured Jean-Pierre when he got a bad stomachache?

   Professor Jones

4. Who introduced Jean-Pierre to a python, dwarf deer, ruffed lemur, and a honey bear?

   Sirima Desjardins

5 Who never got to see Jean-Pierre even though he was to be a guest in her Paris home for two weeks?

   Aunt Louise

Consonant Sounds and Letters

Listed below are twenty words from "The Day Jean-Pierre Went Round the World." At the left of each word is one consonant symbol from the Glossary Pronunciation Key. Underline the letter or letters that spell each consonant sound.

1. **s** seed
2. **s** across
3. **s** absence
4. **s** circus
5. **s** house
6. **z** sneeze
7. **z** islands
8. **f** perfect
9. **f** ruffed
10. **f** elephants
11. **f** laugh
12. **ch** much
13. **ch** watch
14. **sh** seashore
15. **sh** instructions
16. **k** clicking
17. **k** kangaroo
18. **g** gasped
19. **g** guinea
20. **j** luggage

Level 13: "The Day Jean-Pierre Went Round the World" pp. 414-428.

Objective: To identify major and minor story characters. (Comprehension) To identify consonant sound and letter correspondences. (Decoding/Encoding Skills)

Plotting the Action

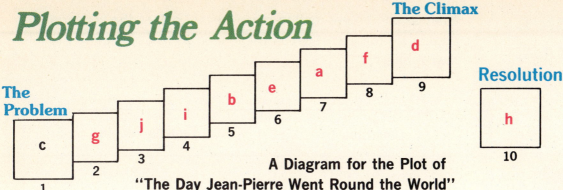

The Climax

The Problem

A Diagram for the Plot of
"The Day Jean-Pierre Went Round the World"

Resolution

Most authors follow a basic plan or **plot** for their story's main events. A simple plot has three important stages: a beginning **problem**, followed by a series of events that rise to a point of **climax**, followed almost immediately by the **resolution** of the problem and the story.

Here are ten events taken from "The Day Jean-Pierre Went Round the World." The first main event is the **problem** that must be resolved by the major characters before the story is over. The **problem** for Cecile and Jean-Pierre is stated in **c. Cecile discovers Jean-Pierre is missing.** Which event describes the moment of **climax** when the suspense is at its highest and the **problem** is about to be resolved? Write the letter of this event in box 9. Then look for the event that immediately follows and provides the **resolution** to the story. Write the letter of this event in box 10. Now see if you can arrange the remaining story events in correct order by writing their letters in boxes 2 through 8.

EVENTS IN "THE DAY JEAN-PIERRE WENT ROUND THE WORLD"

a. Cecile learns Jean-Pierre has eaten many exotic foods.

b. Cecile learns that Jean-Pierre has performed in a circus!

c. Cecile discovers Jean-Pierre is missing!

d. Fifteen people come rushing out at the Nice airport and are about to open the baggage compartment of an American jet.

e. Cecile receives Y.A. Chin's cablegram from Hawaii.

f. Jean-Pierre gets sick in New York City and spends five days with Professor Jones.

g. Cecile receives Sirima's letter from Thailand.

h. Cecile and Jean-Pierre are reunited after a separation of fourteen days and many thousands of miles!

i. Cecile receives Flippo's phone call from Australia.

j. Cecile learns Jean-Pierre is staying with a python, a dwarf deer, a ruffed lemur, a honey bear and an elephant!

Level 13: "The Day Jean-Pierre Went Round the World" pp. 414-428.

121

Objective: To identify the basic stages of the story plot and the correct sequence of events. (Comprehension/Literary Skills)

YOUR STAMP OF APPROVAL

Stamps can be grouped in many ways. Look at the collection of stamps on this page. Group these stamps by completing the following chart.

Countries	Famous People
New Zealand	Amelia Earhart
Maldive Islands	John Muir
Monaco	Emily Dickinson
Dominican Republic	

It is a great honor to be selected as the subject of a stamp. Suppose you were on the postal committee to design some of the many new United States stamps for the coming year. Knowing these stamps would be seen by millions of people in America and around the world, *who* and *what* would you select to represent the following categories? (You may suggest several candidates for each classification.)

CATEGORY	POTENTIAL POSTAL PICTURES
People	Answers will vary.
Places	
Plants	
Animals	
Sports	
Hobbies	
Transportation	
Communication	

Level 13: "Stamp Album" pp. 429-433.

Objective: To categorize things according to their common features. (Study Skill)

WORD DETECTIVE

What words do you think are missing from the sentences in the paragraphs below? Fill in the blanks with words that make the best sense for each sentence.

If you decide to collect stamps, you have to _____choose_____ from the many

different kinds that are available. You _____need_____ to decide if you want

to collect new or _____used_____ stamps.

You can get information about new stamps from _____the/your_____ post office.

Postal workers can tell you what new _____stamps_____ are being issued and

the first day they will _____be_____ available for sale.

Old stamps are much easier and _____less_____ expensive to collect. Ask

your family and friends to _____save_____ old envelopes and post cards with

stamps on them. _____You_____ can remove stamps from envelopes and

post cards by _____soaking_____ them in water until they slip off. Then you

_____can_____ put the stamps in your album.

Very old rare _____stamps_____ can be bought from stamp dealers. These can

be _____very_____ expensive to collect and hard to find. If you are

_____just/only_____ beginning to collect stamps, you probably won't want to

_____collect/buy_____ rare expensive stamps.

There are so many _____types/kinds_____ of stamps to collect in this interesting, educational hobby!

Level 13: "Stamp Album" pp. 429-433.

Objective: To use the Cloze procedure to identify missing words using contextual and grammatic clues. (Comprehension)

WORDS IN FLIGHT

One common way to add words to a language is to use old words in new ways. Another way is to combine old words to make new words.

Here is a group of words about aviation that were borrowed from other areas. Organize the words by writing them in the correct list below to show where the words came from.

pilot	propeller	takeoff	navigator	runway	cockpit
taxi	wing	solo	tail	belly	nose
landing	captain	diving	cruising	cabin	log

Borrowed from words about:

Boat travel pilot, landing, propeller, captain, cabin, navigator, cruising, cockpit, log

Sports takeoff, runway, diving

Animals wing, tail, belly, nose

Car travel taxi   **Music** solo

Many aviation words are **compounds** made by adding the word *air* to other words. Write as many as you can think of. Then use a dictionary to find more.

airplane airport, airstrip, airlines, airliner, aircraft, airfield, airsick, airway, etc.

What other aviation words do you know that name parts of a plane or parts of an airport?

Possible answers: engine, fuselage, wing flaps, rudder, throttle, control tower, terminal, hangers, etc.

On a separate sheet of paper draw a diagram of an airplane or of an airport and label it with as many of the above aviation words as you can. You may wish to use an encyclopedia or other book on aviation for added information.

Level 13: "Daring Flier" pp. 436-439.

Objective: To increase a specialized reading vocabulary relating to aviation. (Comprehension)

Careful Reading and Thinking

Read each of the sentences below. Decide whether the sentence is a statement of fact or an opinion of the writer. If it is a fact, put an **F** on the line in front of the sentence. If it is an opinion, put an **O** on the line. Then write answers to the questions that follow.

___F___ 1. Like jazz, Armstrong was born in New Orleans, Louisiana.

    a. Would it be possible for the writer to prove this statement? __yes__

    Explain your answer. _The writer could obtain a copy of a birth certificate_ _or another official document with the name of the musician on it._

    b. What musical instrument is this jazz musician famous for playing? _Trumpet_

___O___ 2. Perhaps the rock paintings were once part of a special ceremony.

    a. One word in this sentence gives a strong clue as to whether the writer thinks of the statement as a fact or as opinion. What is that word? _Perhaps_

    b. Could the writer prove this statement? _No_

    Explain your answer. _There are no written records of prehistoric man._

    c. What kind of art is being discussed in this sentence? _Cave painting_

___F___ 3. Veterinarians, or animal doctors, take care of sick animals.

    a. What is one book you could use to find out if this sentence gives a fact or an opinion? _a dictionary, an encyclopedia, a nonfiction animal book,_ _a career book._

    b. What is the title of this selection that tells about caring for animals? _"Animal Lovers"_

___O___ 4. Amelia Earhart was the greatest pilot of all time.

    a. Can this statement be proven? _No_

    Explain your answer. _It is a matter of opinion who is the greatest._ _Great means different things to different people._

    b. Some people might disagree with this statement. On a separate sheet of paper write a few sentences explaining why Amelia Earhart might not be considered the greatest pilot of all time. (Answers will vary.)

Level 13: "Daring Flier" pp. 436-439.

Objective: To distinguish between examples of fact and opinion.

USING ADJECTIVES

Adjectives are words that describe nouns. In a sentence one place where you may find adjectives is in a noun phrase.

Noun Phrase
Determiner + *Adjective* + *Noun*

The		spiders
The	greedy	spiders
	Greedy	spiders

A. Use words from the boxes to complete the noun phrases.

Determiners	
A	Some
The	Many

Adjectives		
terrific	silly	graceful
fabulous	funny	enormous

Nouns	
giraffe	ant
storm	dog

Answers will vary.

1. A ___fabulous___ party
2. The ___graceful___ acrobat
3. ___Some___ ___silly___ porcupines
4. The ___enormous___ ___giraffe___
5. A ___terrific___ ___storm___

B. You can combine two sentences that have the same noun phrase when one sentence has a "be" word and an adjective.

The clown caught the rabbit. The clown is long-legged.
The long-legged clown caught the rabbit.

Combine the following pairs of sentences in this way. Find the adjective in the second sentence. Put it in the noun phrase of the first sentence.

1. The hammer cracked the plaster. The hammer is heavy.
   The heavy hammer cracked the plaster.

2. The fish darted through the seaweed. The fish is silver.
   The silver fish darted through the seaweed.

3. The snow covered the bush. The snow is fresh.
   The fresh snow covered the bush.

4. The door slammed shut. The door is broken.
   The broken door slammed shut.

5. The library opened early. The library is new.
   The new library opened early.

Level 13: "Daring Flier" pp. 436-439.

Objectives: To identify the usual position of adjectives in a sentence. To construct a sentence with an adjective before the noun by combining a sentence consisting of a form of "be" plus an adjective with another sentence. (Language Skills)

CAREERS IN AVIATION

Reread pages 440-441. Then decide which of the following people in aviation are described by the sentences below. Write the number of the aviation career in front of the appropriate sentence. Some sentences may apply to more than one career.

1. mechanics	2. dispatchers	3. air-traffic controllers	4. meteorologists
5. pilots	6. copilots	7. flight engineers	8. flight attendants

People working in this career . . .

___8___ work mainly in the cabin of the plane.

_5, 6, 7_ work in the cockpit of the plane.

_2, 3, 4_ work in the control tower.

___1___ work with the planes on the field or in the hangars.

___3___ use a radar screen to help guide planes in and out of the airport.

___7___ keep the flight log, examine instruments in the cockpit, and check out the airplane parts.

___1___ repair and refuel planes so that they are safe to fly.

___8___ see to all passenger needs while the plane is in flight.

___2___ plan schedules, watch weather, and help pilots with their course of flight.

___4___ predict weather by using maps and charts.

___6___ assist pilots in flying the planes.

___5___ are captains in charge of the flight crew.

Match these words from aviation careers with their meanings.

1. _c_ altitude   **a.** group of people working together

2. _e_ forecast   **b.** supply with fuel

3. _f_ cockpit   **c.** height above ground

4. _a_ crew   **d.** record of the flight

5. _d_ log   **e.** prediction

6. _b_ refuel   **f.** place where pilots sit

Level 13: "Careers: Sky High" pp. 440-441

Objectives: To recall details about the information given in a selection. To increase a specialized vocabulary relating to aviation. (Comprehension)   127

A Rule for Laughter: Expect the Unexpected

We have seen that humor is often the result of unexpected and unlikely events. Ilse Kleberger's "The Would-Be Cowboy" is another story with many humorous moments. See if you can complete each of the following incidents from the story by adding the unexpected and unlikely elements that produce both surprise and amusement for the reader.

It was not expected or likely . . .

1. that a woman of Oma's age and dignity would suggest earning her way to America by <u>signing on</u> board ship as a galley cook!

2. that two would-be travelers about to make a long voyage from one continent to another would get lost as soon as <u>they got off the train not far from home.</u>

3. that Oma, a sensible and ladylike grandmother, would pack along with her nightdress, toothbrush, soap, cookbook, and wild birdseed, her <u>rollerskates!</u>

4. that Oma, a fine cook of such favorites as macaroni pudding, would pack a picnic lunch of <u>ship's biscuit and lukewarm water!</u>

5. that Jan, who was normally timid and who had already expressed concern about the bull, would try to <u>lasso it!</u>

6. that Oma, having little experience in the art of bull-fighting, would be able to keep the bull from charging by <u>opening and closing her umbrella!</u>

7. that Jan, who had run away from home that morning, would hear his mother greet their return with the strange question, <u>"Well, did you enjoy yourselves?"</u>

Level 13: "The Would-Be Cowboy" pp. 442-454.

Objective: To identify the aspect of surprise in creating humor. (Comprehension)

An Ounce of Prevention

Things that happen to us are often the result of actions we have taken or *not* taken at an earlier time. In "The Would-Be Cowboy," we find many things happening to Jan and Oma because they either prepared (as Oma) or failed to prepare (as Jan) for their trip. After each of the following sentence parts in **A.**, write the letter of the sentence part in **B.** that tells what happened **because** of Oma's and Jan's earlier actions.

A. Early Events (The Causes)

1. Because Jan hadn't studied his geography, __c__

2. Because Oma knew the importance of letting Jan learn his own lesson, __e__

3. Because Oma included such heavy items as a cookbook and rollerskates in her suitcase, __d__

4. Because Jan hadn't remembered to pack a lunch, __a__

5. Because Oma wanted to prepare Jan for some of the hardships of ocean travel, __g__

6. Because Jan was intent on preparing himself to be a good cowboy, __b__

7. Because Oma knew Jan had learned his lesson, __f__

B. Later Events (The Effects)

a. he was very happy when Oma said she had lunch in her handbag.

b. he forgot he was throwing his lasso at a real live bull!

c. he didn't remember the direction of Hamburg from Eberbach.

d. Jan's right arm grew numb from the weight.

e. she couldn't remember her geography either.

f. she kindly suggested they postpone their trip for a while.

g. she had only packed ship's biscuit and lukewarm water.

Level 13: "The Would-Be Cowboy" pp. 442-454.

Objective: To identify cause and effect relationships. (Comprehension)

129

The Sailmaker or the Sea Captain?

Sailmaker James Forten and sea captain Paul Cuffe share many **similarities** in their life stories. There are also a few important **differences** in their backgrounds and beliefs. Read the following sentences. If a statement is true of the **Sailmaker,** put an X under the heading **SM**. If it is true of the **Sea Captain**, put an X under the heading **SC**. If the statement is true of both men, put X's under both headings. Be sure you can locate evidence in the selection for each of your answers.

	SM	SC	
1.	X	X	was a Black American who lived in the last half of the 18th century.
2.	X	X	was captured by the British during the Revolutionary War.
3.	X		was educated in a public school.
4.		X	was educated with the help of friends.
5.	X	X	had an occupation connected with the sea.
6.	X	X	became quite successful in his work.
7.		X	owned his own business.
8.	X		worked his way up from apprentice to foreman.
9.	X		believed the best hope for Black Americans was to stay in America.
10.		X	believed that the best hope for Black Americans was to return to Africa.
11.	X	X	worked to gain freedom and justice for all Black Americans.
12.	X	X	worked to "cultivate a love for all people."

Level 13: "The Sailmaker and the Sea Captain" pp. 458-464.

Objective: To identify similarities and differences in two historical figures. (Comprehension)

Story Vocabulary, Synonyms, and Word Family Members

Read the story words below in their sentence contexts on the given pages. Then decide which word on the right would be the best **synonym** for the story word. Write the number of the story word on the blank in front of its synonym.

page	story words	possible synonyms
458	1. bound	_7_ huge
458	2. kidnapped	_4_ dock
459	3. apprentice	_10_ grow
461	4. wharf	_1_ headed
462	5. expedition	_8_ devoted
463	6. admired	_2_ captured
463	7. vast	_9_ sameness
463	8. influence	_6_ respected
463	9. equality	_3_ trainee; learner
464	10. cultivate	_5_ trip

Match the words in the two rows below which belong to the same word family. Write the numbers of the words in the first row in front of the words in the second row.

1. admired **2.** equal **3.** apprentice **4.** vastly **5.** influence

_3_ apprenticeship _5_ influential _2_ equality _1_ admiration _4_ vast

Choose one word from each of the word family pairs above and write it in the sentences below.

1. James Forten and Paul Cuffe _____ admired _____ each other at once.

2. James Forten gave _____ vast _____ sums of money to the newspaper *The Liberator*.

3. Both Cuffe and Forten believed in _____ equality _____ and fair treatment for Black people.

4. James Forten learned sailmaking by working for an experienced sailmaker as an _____ apprentice _____ .

5. Powerful and wealthy James Forten used his _____ influence _____ to help black Americans.

Level 13: "The Sailmaker and the Sea Captain" pp. 458-464.

Objective: To use synonyms to develop the meaning of story vocabulary. (Comprehension) To identify words from the same word family. (Decoding/Encoding Skills)

BY SEA OR AIR?

Most of the selections you've read so far in Unit 6 have had something to do with airplanes or ships. Write each word in the box under its correct topic heading below.

runway	anchor	sailmaker	takeoffs	flight crew
aircraft	jet	stevedore	mast	control tower
harbor	Kitty Hawk	airport	mainsail	flight attendant
wharf	whaler	taxiing	cabin boy	ship's biscuits
privateer	wing	schooner	oars	boarding card
waterfront	sails	nose	altitude	flight engineer

Air Travel

runway

aircraft

jet

Kitty Hawk

nose

airport

taxiing

takeoffs

flight crew

control tower

flight attendant

boarding card

wing

altitude

flight engineer

Sea Travel

harbor

wharf

privateer

anchor

whaler

sailmaker

stevedore

schooner

mast

mainsail

cabin boy

ship's biscuits

sails

waterfront

oars

Level 13: "The Sailmaker and the Sea Captain" pp. 458-464.

Objective: To classify selected story words under general semantic categories. (Language Skills)

WORDS FROM A TRUE EXPERIENCE

Find the words below on their listed pages and read them in context. Then write the number of the words in front of the matching short definitions on the right.

page	selection word	short definition
465	**1.** diary	_6_ deep red
466	**2.** stale	_3_ journey by water
467	**3.** voyage	_4_ magnificent; splendid
468	**4.** glorious	_1_ a daily record of one's life; a journal
468	**5.** expectations	_2_ not fresh
469	**6.** crimson	_5_ hopes; dreams; anticipations

 The sentences below tell about events in "Charlotte Forten: Teacher." Each contains an underlined word. Three definitions for this word are given. Decide which definition is the correct one for the word as used in that sentence. Write the letter in front of the sentence.

_b_ **1.** Finally, Charlotte Forten began to get sleepy and found her way to her <u>cabin.</u>
a. small country house.
b. small room below deck on a ship
c. cockpit of an airplane

_a_ **2.** As soon as the first light of morning came, she went up on the <u>deck.</u>
a. platform around a ship
b. to dress or decorate
c. playing cards

_a_ **3.** Together they watched . . . the moon <u>reflected</u> in the water.
a. shining
b. refreshed
c. cool

_c_ **4.** She watched the great white-capped waves as they broke against the <u>bow</u> of the ship.
a. device for shooting arrows
b. one who rows a boat
c. forward part of a ship

_b_ **5.** Charlotte Forten saw a <u>faint</u> strip of dark green on the horizon.
a. timid
b. dim
c. quiet

_a_ **6.** It is far more than my highest <u>expectations.</u>
a. hopes
b. fears
c. sorrows

_b_ **7.** Lightning <u>darted</u> through the clouds.
a. crashed
b. flashed
c. vanished

_c_ **8.** The stewards put mattresses in the passageways so that people would not have to sleep in their <u>stuffy</u> cabins.
a. old-fashioned
b. angry
c. with hot, stale air

Level 13: "Charlotte Forten: Teacher" pp. 465-470.

Objective: To use context clues to develop the meaning of story vocabulary. (Comprehension)

ORDERING EVENTS IN TIME

The sentences below describe events from Charlotte Forten's "Sea Voyage" on pages 466–468. Number the events in the order in which they happened. Write the numbers in front of each sentence.

_5_ The third day a storm comes up and by night the passengers are forced to sleep on mattresses in the passageways.

_3_ Charlotte Forten spends a restless night because of the hot, stale air in the cabin.

_6_ The next morning she struggles up on deck just as someone says, "Land, land, ho."

_2_ As the boat pulls away, Charlotte meets Lizzie Hunn.

_4_ The next day Charlotte Forten and Lizzie Hunn spend the day on deck talking, eating, and watching the sea.

_1_ Charlotte Forten sails from New York for the Sea Islands.

Here are the names and dates of five great sea explorers. Write the names and dates in the proper order on the time line below.

Ferdinand Magellan — 1519–1521: Commanded first voyage to sail around the world.

James Cook — 1768–1779: Explored South Pacific.

Leif Ericson — 1000: Vikings had already settled in Greenland. Evidence that Ericson had reached North American mainland.

Christopher Columbus — 1492: Made his voyage to North America.

Henry Hudson — 1609: Explored Hudson Bay.

TIME LINE

year

```
1000 ——————— Leif Ericson 1000 ———————
  .
  .
  .
1400 ————— Christopher Columbus 1492 —————
1500 ————— Ferdinand Magellan 1519–1521 —————
1600 ————— Henry Hudson 1609 —————
1700
1800 ————— James Cook 1768–1779 —————
```

Level 13: "Charlotte Forten: Teacher" pp. 465–470.
Objective: To identify the sequence of events in a selection. To construct a time line. (Comprehension)

COMPARING LITERARY FORMS

"The Sailmaker and the Sea Captain" may be classified as a **biographical sketch.** Complete the following sentences about biographies and other forms of writing by filling in the missing words.

1. A **biography** is a written story of a person's _____ life.

2. A **biographical sketch** is not as detailed as a complete biography and therefore is much _____ shorter _____ in length.

3. When a person writes a story of his or her own life, it is called an _____ autobiography _____.

4. David _____ McCord _____ wrote about some important events in his childhood in the selection "Until I Was Ten."

5. A **short story** may have a plot that is based on make-believe, but a biography tells about events that are _____ real, true _____.

6. **Essays, biographies** and **articles** are all types of _____ nonfiction _____ writing.

7. **Biographies** are always about _____ people _____, while essays and articles may be about other factual subjects.

8. In this unit we have read prose biographical sketches about four important people: James Forten, Paul Cuffe, Charlotte Forten and _____ Amelia Earhart _____.

9. The selection "The Day Jean-Pierre Went Round the World" would be classified as a _____ short story _____ rather than a biography because Jean-Pierre is a _____ make-believe _____ character.

10. For the same reason as above, the selection _____ "The Would-Be Cowboy" _____ would also be identified as a short story.

Level 13: "Charlotte Forten: Teacher" pp. 465-470.

Objectives: To identify the major characteristics of a biographical sketch. To identify features of a biography in contrast to other literary forms. (Literary Skills)

Organizing with an Outline

One way to organize information to make it easier to understand and remember is by making an **outline**. An outline tells the main ideas and important facts in a selection. Outlines are set up in a way that makes them quick to read and understand.

Read the following selection about the metric system. Then follow the directions given after the selection for outlining the information.

Another Way to Measure

How many yards are there in a mile? How many rods are there in a furlong? You can look up the answers in a book. But can you answer without looking? Not many people can. The figures are too hard to remember. And if you study it closely, this whole system of measurement doesn't make very much sense. Why, for instance, are there 12 inches in a foot but only 3 feet in a yard? Why are there 40 rods in a furlong but only 8 furlongs in a mile?

The system is so confusing that you may wonder where it came from. Much of it came from the ancient Romans. The term *inch,* for example, is from the Latin word *uncia.* The length of an inch was said to be the length of a joint—the joint with the nail—of an adult's thumb. A foot was about the length of a person's foot. And a mile was said to be the distance a Roman soldier could travel in 2,000 steps.

The term *yard* probably has a British origin. According to legend, the length of the yard was decided by King Henry I in the 12th century. A yard was the distance from the end of the king's nose to the tip of his thumb when he stuck out his arm.

Most of the countries in the world use another system of measurement. Its official name is the International System of Measurement Units. But usually it is simply called the *metric system.* In general this system is more sensible and easier to understand than the system we now use in the United States.

The metric system does not operate in peculiar amounts of inches, yards, or rods. Its terms are meters, centimeters, and kilometers, for example. And all of its units may be multiplied or divided by 10. There are 10 millimeters in a centimeter, 100 centimeters in a meter, and 1,000 meters in a kilometer. The foot is the basic unit of our system. The meter is the basic unit of the metric system.

The French created the metric system in 1790. They didn't base the system on the length of a nose, an arm, or a thumb. The metric system was based on the distance from the equator to the North Pole. This distance was divided into 10 million parts. Each part was called a meter.

Before long we, too, will use only the metric system. Learn it now and be kilometers ahead!

(Continued on next page.)

Level 13: "Summer Sleigh Ride" pp. 471-486.
Objective: To organize information by outlining. (Study Skill)

Outlining Information on the Metric System

A. The six headings below might serve as topic headings for paragraphs in the essay "Another Way to Measure," on page 136. Write the headings *in order* beside the Roman numerals.

Our Difficult Measurement System

A Brief Description of the Metric System

The Roman Origin of Some Measurements in Our System

The Origin of the Metric System

An International Measurement System

The Possible British Origin of a Measurement in Our System

I. Our Difficult Measurement System

II. The Roman Origin of Some Measurements in our System

    A. Answers will vary.

    B. _____

III. The Possible British Origin of a Measurement in our System

IV. An International Measurement System

    A. Answers will vary

    B. _____

V. A Brief Description of the Metric System

VI. The Origin of the Metric System

    A. Answers will vary

    B. _____

B. Find the headings for II, IV, and VI in the outline above. Under each heading, write two facts you learned about that topic.

Level 13: "Summer Sleigh Ride" pp. 471-486.
Objective: To organize information by outlining. (Study Skill)

137

Fact or Opinion?

An opinion is someone's own attitude or reaction or judgment about something. It may or may not be based on facts. Reread the essay about the metric system on page 136. Then write **F** by each statement that is fact. Write **0** by each statement that gives an opinion.

F 1. Our term *inch* comes from the Latin word *uncia*.

F 2. The French created the metric system in 1790.

O 3. Our whole system of measurement doesn't make very much sense.

F 4. There are 8 furlongs or 1,760 yards in a mile.

O 5. The system we use in the United States is so confusing that you may wonder where it came from.

O 6. The metric system is more sensible and easier to understand than the system we now use in the United States.

F 7. The *meter* is the basic unit of the metric system.

F 8. There are 10 millimeters in a centimeter.

O 9. Basing a measuring system on the length of a thumb joint was a clever idea.

F 10. The distance from the equator to the North Pole is the basis of the metric system.

F 11. Most countries in the world use the metric system.

O 12. The United States should change over to the metric system immediately.

O 13. King Henry's nose was too short.

F 14. The foot is the basic unit of our system.

F 15. International System of Measurement Units is usually called by its shorter name, the metric system.

Level 13: "Summer Sleigh Ride" pp. 471-486.

138   **Objectives:** To distinguish between fact and opinion. (Comprehension)

SKILLS IN REVIEW

Sounds and Spellings

Here are five pronunciation symbols from your Glossary Pronunciation Key on page 490.

$$\bar{\imath} \quad \ddot{u} \quad \bar{a} \quad \bar{o} \quad \bar{e}$$

Each group of words below has one of these vowel sounds. Write the correct symbol on the line above each group of words. Then underline the letters in each word group that spell the sound.

1.   ā
   aim   came   acorn   day

2.   ē
   eat   meet   hurry   cream   baby

3.   ī
   line   sigh   cry   pie   tiger

4.   ō
   boat   home   total   low

5.   ü
   soon   flute   blue   grew

Words and Word Parts

Find a word in the box to fit each of the word patterns listed below. Write the word parts in the correct spaces.

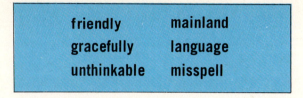

friendly	mainland
gracefully	language
unthinkable	misspell

Word Patterns

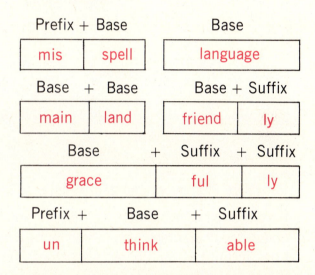

Prefix + Base

mis	spell

Base

language

Base + Base

main	land

Base + Suffix

friend	ly

Base + Suffix + Suffix

grace	ful	ly

Prefix + Base + Suffix

un	think	able

Sentences and Sentence Parts

Find a sentence for each of the sentence patterns below. Write the words in the proper spaces. Det. = determiner, adj. = adjective, adv. = adverb, aux. = auxiliary, pro. = pronoun.

Little children like big toys.
I borrowed some great books.
The year has quickly passed.

1. det. + noun + aux. + adverb + verb

The	year	has	quickly	passed

2. adj. + noun + verb + adj. + noun

Little	children	like	big	toys

3. pro. + verb + det. + adj + noun

I	borrowed	some	great	books

Level 13: Unit 6 Review

Objectives: To identify spellings for the sounds /ay/, /uw/, /ey/, /ow/, and /iy/. To distinguish base words from affixes and other base words. To identify parts of a sentence and their position in a sentence pattern. (Decoding/Encoding Skills)

139

LOOKING BACK...

Here are seven titles from selections in Unit 6, "To Catch the High Winds." The chart below helps us classify each piece according to the kind of writing it is. Write the numbers of the titles in the correct spaces.

Selection Titles

1. "The Day Jean-Pierre Went Round the World"
2. "Daring Flier"
3. "CAREERS: Sky High"
4. "The Would-Be Cowboy"
5. "The Sailmaker and the Sea Captain"
6. "Charlotte Forten: Teacher"
7. "Summer Sleigh Ride"

Kinds of Writing

FICTION		NONFICTION	
realistic short story	fanciful short story	biographical selection	informative selection
1, 4	7	2, 5, 6	3

Imaginary Characters and Real People

Here is a list of characters from the fiction selections in our unit. Match the characters and story titles by writing the number of the titles in front of the characters names. Then write the names of the characters in the appropriate sentences that follow.

Fictional Characters

4	Jan	1	Aunt Louise	7	Polly	4	Oma
7	Emilie	7	Margaret	1	Cecile	7	Jeems

1. ___Jeems___ took care of the museum of the twentieth century where Emilie, Margaret, and Polly found themselves.

2. ___Aunt Louise___ lived in a tall old house in Paris where the Durands came to visit every summer.

3. ___Jan___ wanted to go to America and become a cowboy.

4. ___Oma___ helped teach her grandson a lesson about the hardships of travel.

5. Jean-Pierre was the pet of ___Cecile___, who loved him dearly and worried about him when he had an unexpected trip.

Objectives: To identify literary genre of selections. (Literary Skill) To identify characters from selections. (Comprehension)

Here is a list of real people from the nonfiction selections in Unit 6. Match them with the correct title by writing the numbers of the titles in front of the people's names. Then write their names in the appropriate sentences that follow.

Nonfictional People

_6_ Lizzie Hunn   _5_ Paul Cuffe   _5_ James Forten

_6_ Charlotte Forten   _2_ Amelia Earhart

1. _____Amelia Earhart_____ was the first woman to fly solo across the Atlantic Ocean.

2. _____Paul Cuffe_____ was the captain of whaling ship.

3. _____James Forten_____ made a fortune as a sailmaker.

4. _____Lizzie Hunn_____ met Charlotte Forten on the ship traveling to the Sea Islands.

5. _____Charlotte Forten_____ kept a diary about her work in the Sea Islands.

Now Complete This . . .

Read the paragraph below. Then fill in each space by circling the letter of the word that best fits the meaning of the paragraph.

A person who wants to travel has many kinds of transportation to choose from. Airplanes, boats, trains, buses, cars and bicycles are all popular forms of travel. And, of course, there is always walking!

The type of transportation people choose depends on how far they want to go, how fast they want to get there, and how much _____(1)_____ they want to spend. Walking is probably the least expensive way to travel, but it is also the slowest, especially for long distances. Flying by jet is one of the more expensive ways to travel but it is the _____(2)_____ way to go.

1. a. effort   (b.) money   c. energy

2. a. hardest   b. lightest   (c.) fastest

Level 13: Unit 6 Review
Objective: To recall significant details from the selections. To use the Cloze procedure to identify missing words using contextual clues. (Comprehension)

141

WORDS FROM OUR TRAVELS

Here is a list of headings for the Unit 6 word groups that are printed below. Decide which headings go with each word group. Then write the letter of the heading on the line above the words.

Word Group Headings

a. New Friends for Jean-Pierre
b. Parts of an Airplane
c. Aviation Careers
d. In Jan's Atlas
e. Parts of Paul Cuffe's Ship
f. Colors of a Sea Islands Sunset
g. Jeems' Causes for Worry

Unit 6 Word Groups

1. __d__
Rocky Mountains
Iller River
Lech River
Isar River

2. __c__
pilot
copilot
flight engineer
meteorologist

3. __g__
disease
smallpox
sickness
epidemic

4. __a__
elephant
pig
python
deer

5. __b__
nose
tail
wing
cockpit

6. __f__
rose
golden
crimson
red

7. __e__
cabin
mast
mainsail
ropes

In each of the word groups above, one word is slightly different from the other three in some way. The sentences below help explain how that one word is unlike the others. Decide which word in each group is different and underline it. Then complete the sentences. Answers may vary.

a. Group 1 lists three German rivers and one _____mountain range_____.

b. Group 2 lists three people who fly an airplane from the cockpit and one who _____
studies weather from the control tower_____.

c. Group 3 lists three general words for *illness* and one _____kind of illness_____.

d. Group 4 lists three four-legged animals and one _____legless animal_____.

e. Group 5 lists three aviation words borrowed from animal body parts and one aviation word _____borrowed from sea travel_____.

f. Group 6 lists three shades of red and one _____golden_____.

g. Group 7 lists three parts of a ship used for sailing and one part _____
used as living space for passengers and crew_____.

Objective: To identify and describe semantic similarities and differences with groups of story words. (Language Skills)